THE UNDEFEATED ATHLETE

Michael McCree

McCree, Michael.
The Undefeated Athlete: How to Be a Champion in Any Sport/ by Michael McCree.
ISBN: 979-8-218-07269-8
1. Sports- Children's and Youth Sports
2. Sports- Psychological
3. Sports- Coaching
4. Sports- Parenting

Printed in the United States of America

Special Thanks

I would like to thank my mother, Carrie, for her relentless efforts and love throughout my own amateur athletic journey and life in general.

I want to thank Eric Simmons, who served as Creative Visionary on this project. Eric had a successful collegiate career at the Division-1 level as a basketball player and has raised three Division-1 collegiate athletes. He's also gained worldwide recognition for getting his self-published books into libraries globally.

Other Works by the Author:
- **Gamechanger: The Baseball Parent's Ultimate Guide**
- **The Mind of a Superior Hitter: The Art, Science and Philosophy**
- **The Mental Mastery of Hitting in Baseball** (Film on DVD and Stream)

Table of Contents

"JUST BELIEVE IN YOURSELF. EVEN IF YOU DON'T, PRETEND THAT YOU DO, AND AT SOME POINT, YOU WILL."

—VENUS WILLIAMS

CHAPTER 1
INTRODUCTION

You are in control of your success. However, to become an undefeated athlete with the heart of a champion, you must start to _**think**_ and _**act**_ like one. This book isn't about winning a championship with your team to be considered a "champion." Instead, it's about becoming a champion in your thought, speech, and action. Having a winning attitude, good character, and being a leader are all characteristics of a champion!

This book is entitled _THE UNDEFEATED ATHLETE: HOW TO BE A CHAMPION IN ANY SPORT_ for a specific reason. The words **UNDEFEATED** and **CHAMPION** are intended to stand out to you the most.

The word UNDEFEATED is representative of the mindset you must have to transform yourself as an athlete. An unbreakable, relentless, and mentally tough attitude to overcome all the challenges that will test you on your journey. You will likely experience setbacks, as most athletes do at some point, but if you decide never to give in, you will not be defeated by them.

The word CHAMPION involves conquering things such as negative thoughts, the temptation to procrastinate, and the urge to complain about things an athlete may not like. It's about being victorious over your shortcomings and weaknesses.

Your path to becoming an UNDEFEATED CHAMPION may not be easy, but it's certainly worth it. How you approach the process is EVERYTHING. Each athlete's journey will look different, and yours will be unique from anyone else.

"THE HARDER THE BATTLE, THE SWEETER THE VICTORY"

- LES BROWN

In this book, you will be coached on how to navigate your journey. There WILL be ups and downs. You should *always* expect challenges along the way. Remember that the challenges make the victories much sweeter and that anything worth having is worth working for. There will be some wins and some losses. During competitive events, you will make some great plays and some mistakes. How you handle these ups and downs can be critical to your success.

Elite athletes worldwide, regardless of the sport, separate themselves from the rest because their mindset is on a different level. They possess a "thought process" that drives them to do the necessary work to achieve their goals. As a result, they can keep going when they run into obstacles. Instead of seeing mistakes as "failures," they view them as **_opportunities_**!

Sports provide an excellent opportunity to see what you are made up of on the "inside." Some call it "intestinal fortitude." Sports can test you in ways that other areas of life may not. The mental and physical tests you may experience in sports can shape you forever – and in many cases, perhaps, for the better. **How you decide to _respond_** can and will shape you also.

Studies reveal that former student-athletes (who participated in sports in high school and college) are more likely to be hired for jobs after graduation. What would be your guess as to why this could be? The main reason identified is that sports help to develop people in the area of transferable skills.

Transferable skills are habits learned or developed in one thing that can be useful in other areas of life. The following are just some of the critical characteristics that studies have found that athletes tend to develop while playing sports that can help in many different areas of their life:

1. **Being able to handle constructive criticism -** Athletes are known to take criticism and critique from coaches as necessary information to help them improve. In contrast, others may see criticism as an attack from an authority figure (boss or supervisor).

2. **Time management skills -** Athletes spend hours and hours on the practice field, traveling for games, etc. During all this, especially at the youth/ teen age level, they are also asked to complete schoolwork on time, study for tests, etc. As a result, many athletes have developed the ability to manage their time and juggle their academic and other responsibilities. Usually, in all cases, athletes are required to keep up their grades and fulfill their other obligations to continue playing their sport.

3. **Being a team player and working well in groups** – Athletes are accustomed to being a part of a team. Being part of a team provides an athlete with a greater sense of team-mindedness, which helps them to be able to work with different types

of people in various ways to help achieve a goal.

4. **Fast and adaptable learners -** Athletes are often asked to regularly remember plays or situational team plans. Having to learn and implement new skills in pressure situations is a rare ability. Athletics is one of the few environments that allows a person to exercise these qualities. The capability to learn a new concept quickly is one of the most valuable transferable skills imaginable.

5. **Mental toughness -** Having to earn a position on the team, running/conditioning, pushing themselves to the limit during a workout to get in shape for a sport, and experiencing what it's like to win and lose, are all ways that athletes build their mental toughness. In addition, it has been found that those who have developed their mental toughness through sports are often better equipped to handle real-life situations that will also require mental toughness.

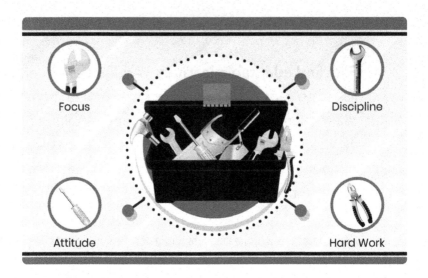

Focus

Discipline

Attitude

Hard Work

The above are identified characteristics from playing sports that are potentially available for you to add to your toolbox in life and use when needed.

THE PROCESS

proc·ess[1]

/ˈprä ses, ˈprō ses/

a series of actions that you take in order to achieve a result.

If your goal is to rise to new heights athletically, you're going to have to fall in love with the process, not just the outcome. Everyone wants the "outcome" and recognition of being viewed as a "champion." Unfortunately, not everyone is willing to do what it takes consistently to get there. This is where YOU, as an athlete, can have the advantage because most are not willing to do it. Your consistency is where you can gain an edge over your competition. YOU are your competition. True champions compete against themselves daily, trying to outdo what they did yesterday. They spend little time focusing on what others are doing, which is something they can't control.

Once you get to the point where you enjoy what it takes to become the athlete you strive to be, the work it takes to get there doesn't seem so difficult. If you learn to love the hard work and dedication itself, not just the glitz and glamor of what comes from it, then you will be on the road to becoming a success in your sport.

TALENT

If you are already very talented, don't rely only on your talent level. Yes, you can appreciate it, capitalize on it and use the talent you've been blessed with to the best

of your ability, but don't *rely* entirely on it alone. Why? Any athlete who intends to get to a higher level cannot rely on just talent because it takes *more* than natural ability to reach full potential. Unfortunately, many gifted athletes don't achieve their goals because they believe that all they have to do is merely show up to the game or practice with *only* their talent, thinking it will do the job. They may believe that talent alone will be good enough to get them where they want to be. It may work for them for some time, but it will not sustain them in the long term.

If you do happen to "make it" to a certain level off, mainly your talent, you will eventually be unable to stay there very long. Your talent should be the extra icing on the cake and work in conjunction with your leadership, attitude, and being a great teammate. Your talent should not be the "end all." Plenty of talented athletes throughout history have fallen short of what they were capable of simply because they did not take full advantage of their capabilities. They may have gotten used to dominating their sport early and figured they could relax. But this mentality won't help you get *better*, no matter how talented you are. The goal is always to be a better YOU.

"HARD WORK BEATS TALENT WHEN TALENT DOESN'T WORK HARD."

HAVING FUN

It would not be truthful to say that winning isn't more fun than losing, but having fun doesn't always come down to the outcome or score. As an athlete, especially those of you at a youth age, remember that one of the most important motivators in sports is *fun*. Also, there is no denying that part of having fun is having *success*. Of course, when you are performing well and helping your team have a better chance of winning, the experience is much better than if you are not. Everyone wants success in their sport, but are they willing to work for it? So the question is, are YOU willing to work for it?

"YOU DREAM. YOU PLAN. YOU REACH. THERE WILL BE OBSTACLES. THERE WILL BE DOUBTERS. THERE WILL BE MISTAKES. BUT WITH HARD WORK, WITH BELIEF, WITH CONFIDENCE AND TRUST IN YOURSELF AND THOSE AROUND YOU, THERE ARE NO LIMITS."

—MICHAEL PHELPS

The material you will read will be in the context of sports but contains principles that you can take with you – not just on the playing field of your sport(s), but in life in general. As you read, you will notice a common theme.

We will focus on HOW to think about certain things that will happen along the way. It's not about what happens; it's about how you THINK about what happens. How you *think* will determine how you approach anything in life, and sports are no different. Your mind can be your greatest tool. Unfortunately, it can also be your greatest enemy if you do not use it properly. Which will you choose?

YOU CAN GET BETTER.
YOU CAN GET FASTER.
YOU CAN GET STRONGER.
YOU CAN GET SMARTER.

ALL OF THESE THINGS CAN HAPPEN ONCE YOU DECIDE TO GO FOR IT!

CHAPTER 2
PRACTICE MINDSET

"I WANTED TO MAKE PRACTICE AS DIFFICULT AND AS HARD AS I POSSIBLY COULD SO THAT WHEN I GOT ON THE FIELD ON GAMEDAY IT WAS EASY."

-LARRY FITZGERALD

A thletes who strive to reach their full potential must learn to see practice differently from their competition. True *champion-caliber* athletes view practice sessions as an essential investment of their time. Their investment is intended to yield a positive return, and mature athletes clearly understand that practice isn't about just *spending* time. Therefore, an athlete's practice time should be quality time *invested*.

The more quality time invested in practice, the greater the results will show during game time. It's easy to go to a practice session and "zone out" mentally. Sometimes you may have your mind drift off and start thinking about what you're going to eat after practice, a math test at school that you have coming up in a few days, and many other things that don't have *anything* to do with the practice going on at *that* moment.

If you can't concentrate in *practice*, how will you be able to focus for the entire duration of a real game? While practicing, not only are you focusing on your skills that involve technique, game speed, and all other physical attributes, but most importantly, you are working on the *mental* aspect of your game. Staying "locked-in" mentally and being sure to make adjustments is critical as well. To heighten your level of focus during a game, you need to work on doing this *while* at practice.

To treat practice like a game, you have to send your mind a message that it's time to "get serious." An excellent way to do this is to get ready for practice like you physically would get prepared for a "real game." From paying attention to what you eat and drink to making sure your uniform is on correctly, having your cleats or sneakers tied tight, etc. One of the reasons why many athletes can't get into "game mode" or mindset during an actual game is because they don't prepare the same way in practice as they do for competition. The saying goes, "Those who *stay* ready never have to *get* ready." So, get to practice as early as possible, focus your mind, and prepare your body as if you were getting ready for a real game. This regimen may be mentally tough to do because concentration is hard. But, if it were easy, everyone would be able to do it!

Treating practice with the level of respect it deserves also helps eliminate nervousness during competition when it counts the most. Athletes who are used to being in a *"game mode"* mindset (even if it's just in practice) are less likely to be nervous. They are so accustomed to playing at full speed with maximum concentration and effort that it's nothing new to them when it's time to play a live game.

WHAT'S YOUR GOAL AT PRACTICE?

Every athlete should arrive at every practice with a goal or some goals in mind. They should always think to themselves:

"What am I trying to get out of today's practice?"
"What can I learn to help me become a little better?"
"How can I establish myself as a better leader on my team today?"

Time spent at practice with no real intention of getting better is time wasted. Great athletes don't waste their time or anyone else's. Not only is it not good for you to waste your time as an athlete, but it's also disrespectful for you to waste away the valuable time of the parents and coaches that take the time and energy they devote to you.

GET 1% BETTER EVERY DAY!

You should enter all practices with the idea that you will get better by at least 1 percent (1%) every day. Many will believe that they need to make giant leaps in progress all at one time, which is untrue. If you can get better by 1 percent (1%) every day, eventually, you will look back and see that progressing by 1 percent (1%) every practice eventually led to a monumental change. As an athlete, you never want to overwhelm yourself. The athlete who believes that they must go from a benchwarmer to an all-star in one practice will only frustrate themselves when they realize that it isn't so likely. You would only be lying to yourself and contributing to your frustration later on.

WHY BEING COMFORTABLE AT PRACTICE IS NOT ALWAYS A GOOD THING

It's easy to head out to practice and work on the aspects of our skill sets in which we are *already* good because this makes us feel better about ourselves. For example, if you are great at one particular skill, you may be excited to do that drill at practice because you like the feeling of having success. However, if you are *not* very good at a particular skill and it's time for your team to start working on it during drills at practice, you may let out a deep sigh of disappointment because you are *not* so eager to work on this aspect of your game. **So, you have to develop the inner strength to motivate yourself to do the things that are hard to do when you don't feel like it!**

For example, a basketball player may be great at doing layups, but they hate shooting and practicing free throws because they aren't very good at it. So, they become irritated with practicing free throws. However, it wouldn't be wise for them to spend most of their time practicing *layups* if they know they haven't improved on their *free throws*. So, while practicing free throws may be frustrating, and the failure of not being at their best may be discouraging, it's needed to increase the overall skill level in that area.

For some reason, though, many players don't work on the areas they need to improve. Instead, they'd rather spend most of their time doing repetitions of drills in which they are *already* good. Why? As mentioned earlier, it makes us feel good to do things that we are already good at, regardless if we know that there are other aspects of our skills that we need to improve. It massages our egos when we do things we know we've perhaps already mastered.

ATHLETES WITH A CHAMPION MINDSET FOCUS ON THEIR WEAKNESSES

An athlete is only truly as good as their weak spots. You must identify as best you can your weaknesses and strive *every* day in practice to continue to erase or minimize those weaknesses. No one is perfect, but you should always make it a habit to focus on eliminating as many of your shortcomings as you possibly can. Be *glad* when you or your coach notice a weakness and it is brought to your attention. Simply learning that you have something you need to fix is the first step to eventually eliminating the problem.

GET TO PRACTICE AS EARLY AS POSSIBLE, GET YOUR MIND FOCUSED, AND PREPARE YOUR BODY PHYSICALLY AS IF YOU WERE GETTING READY FOR A REAL COMPETITION.

PRACTICE YOUR LEADERSHIP

Practice can be used to gain better skills in your sport and as an opportunity to work on your *leadership*. True leaders on a team make sure they lead by example so that their teammates can be motivated to have the same level of focus. In addition, they encourage and inspire their teammates in a way that will help *everyone* get better as an entire group.

HIGH-LEVEL ATHLETES GET *EXTRA* PRACTICE

If you wish to be a champion who rises above the competition, you must do extra work outside of regularly scheduled practice. If you only practice during the weekly team practice slots throughout the season, you will only progress at the same rate as your teammates. However, if you expect to be *better* than your competition—whether opponents or teammates—you have to do *more* work outside of team practice. Can you imagine going to school without having any homework? How would that affect your learning progress? Exactly! You would only be *half* the student you're capable of becoming, and without extra practice, you will only be *half* the athlete you are capable of becoming.

Maybe you have a private instructor who helps you with specific things that you need to work on individually.

Perhaps you have a friend(s) that you can partner up with on the off days when the team doesn't have practice so that you two can practice fundamentals at the nearest park. Team practice is for just that-- the *team*. Team practice isn't designed for the individual athlete to work out all their issues. It certainly can help improve, but not to the degree of *maximum* progress. Team practice time is reserved for coaches to go over things that concern the entire team. It could be things like practicing how to run plays properly for basketball and football. For baseball or softball, to highlight a couple of examples, it could be working on how the defense should react when someone on the other team steals a base. Each sport will be different, but the idea of team goals and individual goals being separate from each other is universal and can be applied to *all* team sports.

Having a private instructor could be a huge help. It is pretty similar to having a private tutor for school. They can help you with your specific issues, and one-on-one time with them can allow you to ask those questions that you may not have the time to ask during team practice.

WHEN YOU "DON'T FEEL LIKE IT"

Some days you may not feel like going to practice. Every athlete at all levels has faced this at one time or another. You may be tired, sick, or just having a bad day, but if you aim to be a superior athlete, you must learn to be mentally tough during these times. The average athlete will allow themselves to drift off mentally and become unfocused, hoping that they can make it through the practice and that it will be over soon. If you feel this way, there is no need to panic. It's normal. Use it as a challenge to see how far you can dig deep down inside yourself to pull out your best effort. Use it as a time to test your limits and prove to yourself that you can fight through adversity. Remember– even when you don't feel like it, as a leader, your teammates still look up to you and are counting on you.

In 1997, Michael Jordan, someone who most people would consider one of the greatest athletes to have ever lived, played one of the most memorable games in sports history. For a player of his caliber, it wasn't out of the ordinary to have such a great game. However, what made his performance so extraordinary was that he did it during a game while he was extremely sick. He was so ill that it was questionable whether or not he would even be able to play that day (Game 5 of the NBA Finals). Jordan was visibly sick, but with his strong desire to help lead his team to a victory, he was able to push his way through the illness onto a 38-point performance. "It's all about desire," Jordan said. "You have to come out and do what you have to do. I was very weak. At halftime, I told Phil (Jackson) to use me in spurts. Somehow, I found the energy to stay strong. I really wanted it bad."*

* Originally published by the Daily News on Thursday, June 12, 1997; written by Frank Isola

If you are genuinely ill, it doesn't mean you should go to practice. Instead, use this as an example of how vital *willpower* is and how it can be used to push you during difficult times.

Willpower_{noun}

will·pow·er I \ ˈwil-ˌpau̇(-ə)r

The ability to control oneself and the strength to carry out one's plan to reach a goal.

Each time you exercise your willpower, it makes you stronger inside and out. So, exercising your willpower during practice will prepare you if you ever have to use it to push through the pain or tiredness in an *actual* game.

THINK AND REFLECT AFTER PRACTICE

After each practice, you should always analyze how you performed. This "reflection" can help you determine what you can improve on and what you did well. Unfortunately, many athletes leave practice with no idea of what progress has been made. If you aren't taking mental notes of your progress or writing them down, you won't know whether you are getting closer to your goals or not. Since athletes should be focused on their goals, they have to constantly be aware of their performance levels.

JOURNALING

Having a journal to keep track of your thoughts and/or progress can be a true gamechanger. This will encourage you to continue focusing on aspects of your skills that you need to do to improve. You can write things down that you feel like you did well in or what you need to work on after a practice session.

MORE PRACTICE BOOSTS YOUR CONFIDENCE

The more you practice, the more confidence you will have when it truly matters. Simply knowing that you have done more work than most others should help eliminate a lot of nervousness one might feel while in competition. Why do athletes get nervous or anxious? Typically it's because they feel like they might make critical errors or embarrass themselves somehow. Usually, that feeling comes from them knowing deep down that they are not prepared well enough to ensure they won't make many mistakes.

Do you get nervous when you tie your shoe? Of course not! Why is that? Well, because you have done it a gazillion times, right? So being nervous about tying your shoe would seem very silly. The main point is that the more athletes practice certain things, the more confident they become in their ability to do them. This confidence leaves less and less room for nervousness to creep into the mind.

"BEING NERVOUS IS NOT SOMETHING YOU SHOULD BE ASHAMED OF. NERVOUS MEANS YOU CARE, YOU REALLY WANT TO DO WELL."

—PAULA CREAMER

KEEP A BALANCE

Most of this chapter has keyed in on *focus*, and the tone has been non-playful. However, one thing to remember is that practice should be fun!

Champion-caliber athletes know how to make challenging things *fun*. Professional athletes love what they do and have lots of fun doing it. Why? They are one of the best at what they do! But how did they get to that point? Performing well is fun, and everyone wants to perform well. Getting to that point requires lots of discipline and hard work. Have fun, laugh, and joke with teammates (when appropriate). Have gratitude for being able to play the sport(s) you love.

Always keep in mind that you have to have a balance when enjoying a sport. So, have an awareness of the situation.

There is a _time_ and _place_ for everything.

When a coach is talking to the team as a group, that is *not* a time to joke with other teammates. Likewise, when a coach is attempting to show you how to do something correctly, it's not a time for laughing and talking. Please pay attention when it's time to listen, show respect to your coaches, and do not be a distraction to your teammates or allow anyone else to be a distraction to *you* when it's time to get to work.

"YOU ARE NEVER REALLY PLAYING AN OPPONENT. YOU ARE PLAYING YOURSELF, YOUR OWN HIGHEST STANDARDS, AND WHEN YOU REACH YOUR LIMITS, THAT IS REAL JOY."

—ARTHUR ASHE

CHAPTER 3
HOW TO HANDLE FAILURE

No matter how much experience an athlete has, they are bound to make mistakes from time to time. In athletics, those who handle tough times the best will succeed more than others. It's not a matter of *if* you will experience struggles; it's a matter of if you will have what it takes to keep pushing forward once you *do* encounter them.

Failures can range from long-term slumps to short-term errors, but the same positive attitude is necessary to learn and move on from both. After making a mistake, the first thing any athlete needs to do is *manage their emotions effectively*. During times like this, your feelings may want to run wild. They may cause you to feel angry, sad, and embarrassed all at the same time. Whenever you make a mistake, your negative emotions will be knocking at the door of your mind saying, "Let me in, let me in!" As a more mature and advanced athlete with a champion's mindset, you will need the ability to not answer to negative emotions that will come up when you are experiencing failure.

Think about how dwelling on your past mistakes caused you to make even more errors or mistakes afterward. Always remember, you are HUMAN! You are bound to make mistakes from time to time. As humans, we are not perfect. We are not robots. Understanding this, we cannot be hard on ourselves to the point where it is *unrealistic*.

Most of the time, our past failures become distractions for our performance in the future.

We could be so upset about a previous mistake we made that the next play (or a few plays later), we forget to be where we need to be during a particular situation, or we aren't focused on the next opportunity to do something *good* for the team.

Perhaps, your issue may not be a lack of concentration. You may merely be hesitant and just plain *afraid* to make another mistake. No athlete wants to let the team down and feel embarrassed when they make a mistake in front of teammates, coaches, friends, parents, and family who are at the game. No athlete *wants* to deal with this, but if you plan on playing at a high level in the future, you will *have* to learn how to deal with it if it happens.

Remember, athletes that are older, better, and who play at a higher level than you make mistakes. Even your favorite athletes that you may look up to go through times where they have to deal with overcoming failures. The main difference between high-level performers and all others is that high-level performers are more experienced with *quickly* moving past their mistakes. If they weren't good at moving past their imperfections, they would never have been able to make it to where they are.

You may have heard those around you say, "just forget about it," and "move on to the next play." To some degree, that may be helpful. However, you can't learn from past mistakes if you forget them *entirely*. So, when learning from your mistakes during competition, you have to have "skillful remembrance," which means remembering something that happened to help you bring more clarity and focus on the situation while learning from it healthily.

If you're too afraid to look back and unravel your mistakes, it will be too easy for you to repeat them over and over again. Having "selective amnesia" means remembering the valuable part of the mistake and forgetting about the emotional hurt you might have experienced. It would be best to get over your ego to do this successfully.

Surprisingly, people don't usually take your mistakes as seriously as you think they do. They're typically too worried about their own to dwell on yours for too long. Let's say that there are 12 players on the team. All 12 may have committed some mistake during the game. All 12 may think, "Sheesh, I messed up badly today. I wish I had not done that." Each team member, so busy thinking about what THEY did during the game, has very little time to worry about what YOU did. Also, in the future, others usually don't remember the little mistakes that you made. *No one will ponder on your mistakes as much as you will.* That's one crucial thing that we all tend to forget. Our egos want to convince us that the universe revolves around *us* and that everyone is thinking about everything we are doing when it is the opposite.

WHEN YOU DON'T GET THINGS YOUR WAY

"SUCCESS ISN'T OWNED. IT'S LEASED, AND RENT IS DUE EVERY DAY."

J.J. WATT

There are only so many available spots in a starting lineup on a team. This "shortage" means that only a certain number of combinations of players can be placed on the field, as far as position and in the lineup. So, it's safe to say that not every player will get their wish when it comes to when or where they contribute to a team. Example: In baseball or softball, you may be hitting in the 7th spot of the batting order, but you really would like to bat in the 2nd or 3rd spot. You may be playing left field when you feel like you deserve to be playing centerfield. In basketball, you may think you are the best point guard on the team, but the coach gives you more opportunities at the shooting guard position. Whatever the case may be, whatever the sport, there is a right and wrong way to handle these situations.

Handling things the wrong way might include:

Getting Angry - You may feel like you belong in a specific position, but being upset and voicing your anger about a coach's decisions could work against you. There is no reason to get angry about not getting your way. Frustration may come into your mind, but anger will only cause you to think negatively. If you can use your frustration to devise a plan to make things better for you, it will be much more helpful. Always use your emotions to spark some logic to help you start *thinking* your way out of the situation. Tangible solutions to problems, whether in your sports life or life in general, start with *logic.*

Emotions change like the weather, as they say. So don't rely entirely on your feelings to tell you the truth about certain situations. Most importantly, it's *never* good if the coach happens to hear from someone else about anything negative you have said about them or the team. So be sure not to gossip about a coach. Don't make decisions that can affect you long-term because you feel negatively in the short-term.

Gossiping – Sometimes, athletes can be emotionally hurt when they don't get what they want, and many times they will complain about it to other people on the team to see if the others will agree with them. As the old saying goes, "misery loves company." Anytime someone isn't happy with the way things are going for them within a team, they tend to want to spread the negativity they feel to other people, so they don't feel like the only one experiencing the negativity. You should avoid *being* that person, and you should avoid being *affected* by someone like this when you see they are attempting to get you involved.

Developing a False Sense of Privilege - means that you have perhaps convinced yourself that you have earned something that you did *not*. For example, sometimes, we let friends and parents lead us to believe that we deserve a spot or position on the team that we did not earn. It takes inner honesty to realize this because we naturally think we deserve something that isn't owed to us many times. Please take a moment to think about a time in the past when you genuinely felt like you deserved something while at the same time you knew you hadn't worked hard enough to earn it.

Giving Up - Sometimes, the struggle of not having things go your way can lead to confusion, embarrassment, frustration, anger, and perhaps being emotionally drained. These emotions could be the primary ingredients behind making an athlete want to give up because they don't want to have to deal with the feelings of failure anymore. Giving up, however, isn't a good idea because if you *do* quit, you will undoubtedly begin sending *yourself* "subconscious messaging" that you don't have what it takes to overcome obstacles in sports and life. Psychologically, you will be conditioning yourself to bail out when things get tough. In addition, this "subconscious messaging" will make it easier for you to give up on other life situations when they get hard. For example, you could begin conditioning yourself to believe that you won't have to fight and work harder to bring up your grades in school when you don't get off to a great start or that you won't have to stick with the job when your boss needs a project done on short notice as an adult.

Don't run from it!
Learn from it!
Grow from it!

DEVELOP A RESPECT AND APPRECIATION FOR WHAT FAILURE CAN DO FOR YOU.

Now, let's talk about the *right way* to go about a situation when things aren't going your way:

Ask if you don't know - find out what you need to do to get better or to earn the position you want. Don't be afraid to ask coaches about areas of your skills where they can see the need for improvement.

Turn inward - ask yourself what you think you could do better to be in the spot you want to be.

Set a goal - aim to produce more for your team. Become the one who _deserves_ to be in the position that you desire because you add value to the team.

You may find it easy to allow others to make you feel like you deserve a spot that you did not earn fair and square. As parents, your mother and father will always believe that you are worthy, mainly because they are your parents and because they love you. So often, they can get emotional if you don't get your way on a team. It's up to *you* not to be persuaded by your parent's emotions. It's up to you, to be honest about your situation and the personal responsibility needed to change for the better.

You owe yourself before anyone else does!

As mentioned earlier, when things don't go your way, you might feel it's because someone is not giving you something that you think you deserve. Sometimes an athlete might think a coach owes them something in particular. Also, deep down, you may feel like you can just sign up for the team and expect to play where you want to or have the position you want to have.

Expecting to be owed for things you haven't worked for puts you in a vulnerable position. So, always remember that what's "fair" is what you have worked for, and fair playing time is not always equal.

"My coach doesn't let me play in my favorite position. That's not fair."

"How come I don't get to be a starter each game?"

These questions can quickly come into your mind if you don't train yourself to kick these thoughts out of your head when they arise.

NO ONE OWES YOU ANYTHING

Athletes need to get away from the notion that coaches, parents, or teammates owe them things they want. This "owing" could be in the form of praise, trophies, a pat on the back, or a particular position on the field. This is not to say that coaches and parents shouldn't do their jobs to help you in your efforts. It's to say that you shouldn't rely on their efforts to determine whether you will give your all. If you receive large amounts of help from coaches, teammates, and parents, all the better. But it isn't something you should blame as a reason for lack of success.

Athletes may feel like their coaches owe them the playing time they want. They think that their teammates owe them respect as a leader. They may believe that their parents owe them a certain level of support. Of course, you would hope that you get all of these things, but what if you don't?

What if your parent(s) don't support your goals? *Will you give up on them?*

What if your coaches don't see you as capable of playing a particular position on the team? *Will you stop trying to prove to them?*

What if your teammates don't see you as the leader you aspire to be? *Will you then stop doing your best to lead your team?*

Never ask for anyone to give you the respect you deserve as an athlete. Instead, always strive to carry yourself in a fashion that will have you *earn* the respect of others. Earning others' respect includes that of your parents, coaches, and teammates. Trying to force people to give you a certain level of respect, admiration, or attention will only give you a false sense of the reputation you seek.

PLAYING TIME

How often you get to play on your team or at what position is usually determined by the coach. However, it's best to tell yourself that no one else determines what you get but you. If you have this mindset, you will be forced to make no excuses about where you end up on your path.

Be so good; they can't ignore you.

If you are experiencing a lack of playing time, first look at what you can do to change things. Don't look to blame others or make excuses because that is less likely to help you. Thinking that way will force you to feel sorry for yourself, and no person has ever empowered themselves by feeling like this about their situation. Feeling sorry for oneself will make a person less likely to take action because there is nothing more that people who feel sorry for themselves want than to have others feel sorry for them.

When you hope for someone to hand you something that you should have earned through your actions, you give *them* the power to decide how *you* will feel. Your feelings determine your thoughts and your thoughts dictate your behaviors. So, allowing your emotions to be swayed by others could equate to having less control of your destiny. Don't allow others to determine how hard you work. Whether someone else acknowledges your hard work, positive attitude, or skill should be irrelevant to you. Yes, it feels good to be recognized for those things. Of course, receiving compliments is tremendous and acceptable at times, *but* don't allow it to enter your mind and be a reason not to continue pressing forward.

"MY MOTTO WAS ALWAYS TO KEEP SWINGING. WHETHER I WAS IN A SLUMP OR FEELING BADLY OR HAVING TROUBLE OFF THE FIELD, THE ONLY THING TO DO WAS KEEP SWINGING."

—HANK AARON

EXPECT THINGS TO BE TOUGH

There are plenty of circumstances you should expect on your journey. Your expectations set the tone. One major factor that keeps athletes from working hard is that working hard is *tough*. The obstacles to working hard are more *mental* than physical. When going through training for your sport, whether you're performing drills, running, or weight lifting, you will encounter some struggles and may even feel like quitting. These times can be overwhelming mentally and emotionally. However, if you go into the situation knowing that things may get tough for you, you will be less likely to be overwhelmed when "the going gets tough."

THE PEOPLE THAT CARE ABOUT YOU MAY NOT BE ABLE TO HELP ... & THAT'S OKAY!

A challenging notion for many athletes to realize is that not all our family members and close friends will always be able to help us. No matter how much they care, some of them are not equipped to assist in the way that you may need. They may not have been the type of high-level athlete you strive to become. Therefore, they may not have been through the things that high-level athletes go through; thus, they may not be able to contribute to you from an advice perspective, which is okay. Allow those who *can* help you to assist in any way they can.

You have everything it takes to pave your way to success.

"I NEVER LEFT THE FIELD SAYING I COULD HAVE DONE MORE TO GET READY AND THAT GIVES ME **PEACE** OF MIND."

—PEYTON MANNING

CHAPTER 4
DEALING WITH COACHES

You could have many different coaches throughout your athletic career. Each one will be different in style, personality, character, and amount of knowledge they have about the sport in which you're participating. If you're lucky, you will get a coach with a likable personality and good character who knows a lot about the sport and can teach you well. If you are fortunate enough to have a coach like this, chances are you played for someone different previously or ended up having another coach the following year. This dynamic means that you could encounter a situation where you feel challenged in your relationship with your coach. Sometimes you may be challenged in a way that you do not like.

Parents might speak negatively about a coach or multiple coaches you currently have or have had. You might be at the dinner table or on the ride home from a practice or game and have heard a conversation involving your parents saying unpleasant things about your coach. As a superior athlete, you have to stay focused on striving to be the very best you can be. Worrying about something that you can't control will drain your energy and focus. So yes, your parents -- who don't have to step onto the field every game in full focus mode -- may have the time to chit-chat about how much they don't like this or that about a coach. However, YOU must not involve yourself in anything that can take away from what matters the most - your goal(s).

Every coach, regardless of whether you like their personality or style of coaching, could be the one who gives you a bit of crucial information that could help you turn your whole game around for the better. Let's say, for example, you have a coach you don't necessarily like – for whatever reason. You may not like them because they yell at you, and when they do, it makes you uncomfortable. Does this mean that they aren't qualified to give you good information about how you could improve your game?

As long as you play any sport, you will likely encounter a coach you aren't comfortable with, but do not let that cause you to "tune out" that coach's information. That may be one of the worst things that any athlete can do. **Never let your emotions stand in the way of your improvement.** If you get so emotional about a coach that you miss out on ways to get better and improve, you are the one who loses.

On the flip side, don't be so comfy with a coach that it causes you to relax to the point where you don't push yourself to get better. Some athletes rely heavily on motivation from a coach, whether it be:

Negatively motivating - a coach yelling or showing that they are upset.

Positively motivating - a coach who gives lots of compliments and makes you feel good about yourself.

Regardless of the type of coach you have, it's best to rely on your inner motivation. **Don't rely on outside sources to make you want to be great.** If you do, your determination will fluctuate and be at the mercy of whatever the coach's motivation style is in that particular season. Always strive to be a highly motivated player *regardless* of who the coach is. If you do what you are supposed to do as an athlete, you will have a chance to be successful no matter your relationship with a coach.

LEARN AS MUCH AS YOU CAN FROM EVERY COACH

Coaches are human, just like everyone else. Their human quality means they won't be perfect, but you should be able to learn, at the very least, *one* thing from each coach that you encounter. From each coach, you can compile all of the lessons learned and use them for your benefit in the future. A key component of learning is asking questions. **Asking questions is the key to gaining knowledge.** It is crucial to ask coaches questions when you are either confused about a concept they have mentioned or if you have just thought of a question to ask and need clarity.

No matter what, never provide a coach with an opportunity to say anything negative about your character. Your character will consist of:

attitude: being positive vs. being negative
effort: whether you hustle and play/practice hard at all times
coachable: do you take instructions well from the coach?
handles adversity: can you bounce back from mistakes?

HOW TO DEAL WITH COACHES WHEN YOU MAKE MISTAKES

Since everyone makes mistakes, it's clear that you will do something that your coach dislikes at some point in your athletic career. Not every coach reacts to errors the same. Some are more laid back and may talk to you calmly in a "one-on-one" manner. Others may be more loud or passionate with their tone. Some yell and scream, but if you aren't able to deal with it, you may get upset to the point where it affects your performance negatively.

First, you must understand that as an athlete striving to be the best, you will not and cannot allow yourself to stray from the positive mental attitude necessary to play at a high level. So whether you have the most laid-back coach who rarely ever makes a sound or if you have one that everyone can hear in nearby surroundings, it shouldn't stop you from giving your all.

You won't be able to handpick the coach of your choice. So, it would be best to get used to having zero power over who your coach will be for any given team you are on. Athletes want to impress their coaches just as much as they want to please their parents and teammates. This "pleasing" is a natural feeling that any competitive athlete has and is why players experience emotional letdowns whenever they do something that doesn't please the coaches, parents, or team. To add to this feeling, having a coach who yells at you after letting the team down can take you to an even lower frame of mind.

Coaches can be some of the greatest competitors at times. Most of them love to compete so much that even after their playing days, they decided to stay in the sport so that they could still in some way be involved in the competition, which makes sense when it comes to coaches who want to win so badly. If you can fully understand this, it will help you realize that it's not a personal attack on you if they do yell at *you*. Many athletes get so flustered when being yelled at that they assume the coach is yelling at them because they hate or dislike them as an individual. This scenario is usually NOT the case.

I've dealt with coaches who spoke as quietly as a mouse, and I've also played for coaches who would throw tantrums in the middle of games. Yes, it can sometimes be embarrassing to be "chewed out" by a coach in front of others, but don't let it affect you, and remember, this can be a great lesson in life when dealing with others, especially authority figures. Don't always think mom and dad can come to your rescue every time a coach gets on to you. Changing coaches In the high school and college ranks isn't as easy as when you are younger. Younger age groups might have the luxury of choosing different clubs or rec teams from year to year, but high school zoning and district rules will prevent them from changing teams as easily. So many times, you may have to just deal with the situation. This "coping" doesn't mean you should be berated or disrespected as a person by *any* coach, though. If a coach says anything that severely crosses the line of a conversation that a player and coach SHOULD be having, let your parents know so that they can help figure out if it's something worth addressing with the coach. This "information sharing" by no means suggests that you as a player should rely on your parent(s) to come to your rescue in every situation you experience with your coach.

COACHES DON'T LIKE EXCUSES – THEY MAKE MATTERS WORSE

When things don't go our way, we instantly come up with excuses to escape the responsibility we share in the problem. Sometimes, athletes may even use these excuses with their coaches to convey that it's "not my fault." Many coaches hate for their players to make excuses for their mistakes. As a former college athlete, I definitely understand how certain circumstances can occur in a game or practice when we didn't execute something well or a negative play happens that was out of our control. However, even if something that happened wasn't your fault, never make excuses for the play that happened. Whatever the case is, own up to your role in the situation and move on. It doesn't feel good to make a mistake and be criticized in front of others for it; this is very understandable, but making any excuses will not make things any better. In fact, they can make things more troublesome. Not only did you do something you weren't supposed to do, but now you're not taking responsibility for your mistake. This lack of accountability looks even worse than just simply making a mistake in the first place.

While in college, I had an encounter with my coach that taught me a lot. One day, I made a mental mistake on the field, and my coach didn't hesitate to let me know about it. He ran over to me and started questioning why I would have made such a mistake. Let's just say it was *undeniable* that he wasn't too happy about it.

At that moment, I chose not to make any excuses or attempts to justify what I had done. Before he could fully express his disdain for my mistake, I had already acknowledged that the error shouldn't have happened and that I shouldn't have done what I did for a player of my caliber and talent level. I did this without hesitation before he could fully unleash his frustration about what had happened.

Before you know it, he had calmed down, shook his head in agreement, and walked away. I had diffused the situation by taking full responsibility for my actions, and the coach *respected* that. I had told him everything he was getting ready to say to me, which, at that point, really left nothing for him to say. My response was something like this:

"Coach, as a senior, that was a mistake that I shouldn't have made. I'll make sure I concentrate better next time. I'll make sure it won't happen again."

Everyone makes mistakes, but most importantly, my coach appreciated me taking responsibility for the situation. There really was nothing else for him to say after I had given my response.

Think of a time when something similar may have happened to you. Did you wish you could have responded better?

IF YOU DON'T KNOW...ASK!

Never be afraid to approach a coach about anything dealing with what you need to do in a practice or game situation or where you need to be during any given situation. For whatever reason, some athletes hesitate when they are unaware or don't understand how to do something. Not raising questions about things you don't understand will only cause an issue later on for you and

your team. Many athletes will not take the time to go and ask the coach for clarification out of fear they will be judged or embarrassed that they may look like they weren't paying attention.

It's much better to save yourself the embarrassment *in the actual game* than to NOT ask for help when you need specific information. For example, your coach may have taught you a new way of doing something last week, and you may have forgotten quickly, so don't be ashamed to go to the coach and ask them to explain the concept again. Instead, you might say something like, "Hey, coach, could you please explain that again? I'd really like to make sure that I get it right." This "desire to learn" and "get it right" shows an athlete's responsible side, and most coaches will respect this approach and won't mind going over it again.

CHAPTER 5

TAKING YOUR GAME TO THE NEXT LEVEL

Everyone *wants* to take their abilities to the next level, but few will. Why is this? There is a big difference between *wanting* something and *executing* (i.e., taking the necessary steps to achieve something). Wanting and not executing is one of the biggest traps that can keep you on a lower level and prevent you from maximizing your potential. Sometimes an athlete may be just *one* small step away from being able to perform how they would like to but can't seem to get their skills up to that next level. As in any sport, the small things count tremendously in the long run. So, why do certain higher-caliber athletes choose to do the small things that set them apart from the rest of the crowd? One primary reason is that they do not give in to *comfortability*.

"COMFORT IS THE ENEMY OF ACHIEVEMENT"

– DR. FARRAH GRAY

Getting *too* comfortable is a major reason why many athletes end up settling for much less than they can be. As a result, many are unable to step outside their "comfort zone," i.e., they become complacent, and *complacency* is one thing that many former athletes regret when they look back on their careers. Some don't make the definitive choice to elevate their level of performance because it will require that they take action and do things they are not entirely willing to do. This unfamiliar journey to being able to perform at a higher level *consistently* may come with some uncertainty.

Believe it or not, many athletes (no matter the sport) are simply *afraid* to be the athlete they wish they could be, even though they fantasize about it all the time, as most people do. To *become* the athlete, you dream of becoming, you must *act*. Many want to *be*, but few want to *become*. There is a big difference between being and becoming. *Becoming* is going to require **action** and **transformation**.

Yes, it may be hard, in the beginning, to make the transition and start doing what it takes to get to the level that you want to be at, but in the mind of a top-level athlete, it's even harder to allow yourself to be less than what you know you are capable of being. That, too, can negatively affect you. Reflecting on a game or season where you *know* that you could have done much better is a hard thing to do. You would possibly feel as if you have let *yourself* down.

Ultimately, choosing between the "lesser of difficulties" is a decision you must make. Will you choose the initial difficulty of breaking your old habits of mediocrity or of dealing with the *regret* of the results of your mediocrity? Don't subject yourself to "regret" in the future. If you envision your choices this way, it can make it easier to deal with the early stages of feeling uncomfortable from failing when trying new ways of bettering yourself. Being able to withstand the ups and downs on your path is crucial.

Some may feel like quitting when things get hard because perhaps they think that any degree of failure they encounter will make them uncomfortable. However, as soon as they experience a lack of comfort, they will retreat and forget *all* the promises that they've made to themselves to do better.

Once you get past the stage of dealing with being uncomfortable, you often may experience that you have some underlying fears in you. This fear of failing is a major reason many athletes don't even attempt to improve themselves.

LETTING FEAR AFFECT YOU

Fear is one of the most natural emotions there are in humans.

When you focus hard and start to improve yourself, you will see that your improvement is a product of your hard work. Once you see that the more hard work you put in, the better results you get, hard work will no longer be so much of a negative thing. You will be *excited* to practice or work out on your own time when you don't have team practices because you *know* what the end result will bring you. Most athletes fear hard work because they have never seen the effects it can produce for them. However, those who have experienced the benefit of what hard work can do for them have little fear of it. Later in this book *(Chapter 10: Competing Without Fear)*, we will explore more in-depth ways to demystify the concept of fear and overcome it.

USING DISCOMFORT TO YOUR BENEFIT

You may be someone who dreads discomfort. Plenty of people worldwide go out of their way to avoid feeling uncomfortable. Those who figure out how to use this to their advantage are likely rewarded in the end. In many cases, the frustration from your discomfort can be the spark you need to transform yourself. Unfortunately, – it isn't quite enough to be comfortable with your average performance if it doesn't inspire you to change.

Some of the most successful people to ever live went through phases in their life where they felt *so* dissatisfied that it ultimately forced them to decide to change their situation. If you look at your discomfort as a **_wake-up call_** rather than a *problem*, you can quickly change your situation. Don't quit because of the irritation you might experience; choose to make the necessary changes to erase that discomfort. It's possible to use it as a form of motivation. Always know that just because it's possible doesn't mean it will be *easy*. It can be challenging to put down video games or turn off the television and decide to go and train to get better at your skills. Setting aside things you enjoy can be extremely tough to do mentally, but it's at the core of what separates good athletes from *great* ones.

DISCIPLINE IS DOING WHAT NEEDS TO BE DONE, EVEN IF YOU DON'T FEEL LIKE DOING IT

SELF-DISCIPLINE

The importance of self-discipline is often underestimated. Yet, it's the key, missing ingredient for many athletes. After all, everyone knows *how* to be a success. That is not a secret. Most people have the knowledge and information on what it takes to get to where they want to go, but why don't many of them get there? *Self-discipline* bridges that available data with an athlete's desired result. Everyone *knows* you must work hard to improve at whatever sport you participate in. The only thing is that most athletes don't always *feel* like doing the hard work. Even if you have an action plan to help you reach your goal, if you don't have enough grit, focus, and determination to follow through with it, you will stand a lesser chance of attaining your goal.

Here is a question you should always ask yourself:

DO I HAVE THE ABILITY TO OVERCOME MY WEAKNESSES?

PROCRASTINATION

Procrastination is when you constantly put off tasks that you should be completing. It's when you plan to do extra training or some much-needed work on your skills, but you decide to reschedule it for another time – telling yourself that you'll "do it later."

"I'll do it tomorrow."

...turns into...

"I'll do it next week."

...turns into...

"I'll do it next month."

...turns into...

"I regret never doing it."

Procrastination is a silent killer. And unfortunately, it's ultimately a weakness of many people worldwide, not just athletes. **Discipline** is what can prevent this unproductive habit.

Procrastination will say, "It's okay, you will have all the time in the world to do it tomorrow."

Discipline will say, "I can find time to do it today and tomorrow!"

SOMEDAY, I WILL DO IT...."

"_TODAY_ I WILL DO IT!"

Being Stubborn (aka "hard-headed")

You may have heard the term "hard-headed" in the past being used by adults to describe children who don't listen well to adult advice. However, not listening can be especially true for you as an athlete if you are someone who decides that you don't need to listen to your coaches and those who offer practical advice that may help you.

"I don't care what anyone else thinks. I want to do my *own* thing, *my* way!"

Having this type of attitude can be a crucial mistake. As mentioned in chapter 4 on the relationship with coaches, you must be **coachable** and willing to take in helpful information at all times.

COMPARISON TO OTHERS

"WHY COMPARE YOURSELF TO OTHERS? NO ONE IN THE WORLD CAN DO A BETTER JOB OF BEING YOU THAN YOU."

-ANONYMOUS

Comparing yourself to other athletes is natural. Sports revolve around competition, and in competition, there will always be an instinct to compare. The comparison of teams and players occurs by simply observing. One athlete is faster or quicker than another. One may be taller or much more muscular than another one. Although it's natural, the idea of comparison can negatively impact an athlete's mindset if it isn't put into proper perspective.

Comparison to others can make athletes feel like they are less than others, or they start highlighting all negative traits they think they may have. In addition, it causes the athlete to have an external focus – .i.e., being overly concerned about things entirely out of their control.

There is a much more skillful way to gauge your progress based on other athletes in your sport. It's okay to look at others and see what pieces of their game you could borrow and use in your own game.
Here are some usual comparisons that athletes make regarding others:

- How fast another is
- How strong another is
- The level of skill that another has
- The leadership and confidence that another shows during competition

STAY IN YOUR LANE!

Staying in your lane means not spending too much time focusing on what others are doing because it will take the focus away from what **YOU** are doing or need to be doing. The concept of "staying in your lane" is an analogy borrowed from sports like track and field and swimming, where each participant has a designated lane to run or swim in during the race. Track and field sprinters have to stay within the white lines painted on the track. They are taught to run and look straight ahead the entire time, not to the right or to the left, to check and see where their competition is. Why? Because turning their heads to look at other sprinters will cause them to slow down, thus affecting their race time.

There is a famous photo of Olympic swimmer Michael Phelps swimming in a race. In the photo's background, you can see an image of a swimmer in the lane next to him. The swimmer competing against Phelps is seen looking over into Phelp's lane during the race. It's a perfect representation of just what NOT to do when you should be focused on what's taking place in YOUR lane. This concept is not only great to follow in sports, but in life in general.

ONLY SEEK TO CONTROL THE THINGS THAT YOU CAN CONTROL

STUDYING ATHLETES THAT ARE MORE ADVANCED THAN YOU

What would probably be the first thing you do if you want to learn how to be a good break dancer? You would watch it…you would try it yourself…and then you'd watch even *more* to see what adjustments need to be made until you can figure out how to make your moves look like that of the breakdancer you are studying. Would you watch just anybody breakdance? Of course not! You would attempt to find the very best of the best to research and learn from them.

Although it's important not to compare yourself to others in particular ways, learning from those with a more advanced skill set in your sport can provide clues. "Success provides clues!" Find those who are successful at what it is you look to accomplish and piece together the steps for you to follow to get there. With the internet, there are plenty of ways you can watch top-performing athletes. In addition, you can search for videos that are specific to your sport(s). If the only time you're observing athletes playing your sport, and they are your peers of the same age group and skill level, you're only watching those with similar talent. Therefore, it's your peers you're watching and learning from daily. To reach your potential, however, *it's best* to observe those who are better than you.

WHY SETTING GOALS MATTER

One reason many athletes don't reach their potential is that they haven't seriously thought about what type of athlete they would like to be in the future. It may cross their mind. They may even have a general idea of it, but they have no specific characteristics in mind that they would wish to have. The best way to do this is to *list* the goals you want to accomplish in the sport(s) you play. Making a list of goals helps you focus on more *specific* aspects of your journey.

Having your goals written down not only makes you *think* about them more but also forces you to envision them clearly. When you can see something visually on paper, it creates an imprint on your mind that will be hard to forget. Why is this important? Your subconscious mind absorbs all things it sees, hears, and feels. Writing goals down- and even going a step beyond that and reading them aloud- will cover the visual aspect and the hearing aspect, making the connection to become one with your goals even *deeper*.

Be a **3D athlete**, *one who decides, develops, and does!*

Decides - they will do better

Develops - a plan on how to get there

Does - it! The action to get there

Deciding doesn't mean hoping and dreaming. It's making a firm decision that you will become a better athlete. A strong desire for change is necessary.

Developing a plan is much easier for those who have *decided* to change their performance for the better.

Doing it will require strong will and discipline.

THERE ARE TWO PAINS IN LIFE. THERE IS THE PAIN OF DISCIPLINE AND THE PAIN OF DISAPPOINTMENT. IF YOU CAN HANDLE THE PAIN OF DISCIPLINE, THEN YOU'LL NEVER HAVE TO DEAL WITH THE PAIN OF DISAPPOINTMENT.

—NICK SABAN

CHAPTER 6
THE IMPORTANCE OF SETTING GOALS

"A GOAL WITHOUT A PLAN IS JUST A WISH."
— *ANTOINE DE SAINT-EXUPÉRY*

After deciding that you will strive to improve yourself, you should have a **plan** to get there. After all, a goal without a *plan* is only a *wish*. Self-improvement doesn't happen by accident. As mentioned, writing down your goals is a significant first step if you're serious about improving your skill set and reaching new heights. Setting worthy goals gives you a sense of direction. Without direction, it can be challenging to outline what needs to be done to accomplish what you are striving to achieve.

Top performers in various fields are known for stressing just how important it is to have a *clear* outline of your goals. Whether it's millionaire business owners, top-performing athletes, world-famous entertainers, or award-winning musicians, they all have goals they aspire to reach. Most of them will tell you that they write down their plans to see them visually so that the picture of where they want to be is clearer in their minds.

Athletes should write their goals down and read over them often. One important thing to remember is that the goals you choose to write down should be *your* goals, no one else's. So many athletes will adopt *others'* goals as their own. A coach or parent of yours may be able to help guide you in the right direction so that your goals are reasonable. Then again, what's considered "reasonable" in *their* eyes may underestimate what's possible for *you*. You may be more capable of reaching far beyond the goals that someone else has set for you, and if you internalize others' limitations, you may never fully realize these goals. Know the difference between being "reasonable" and underestimating what you are capable of.

A plan for you that is personal to *you* is more likely to generate more positivity surrounding your goals. This

THE IMPORTANCE OF SETTING GOALS

way, they become **yours** *emotionally*. To create an emotional attachment to your goals, **envision** the joy and excitement of reaching the goals that you set for yourself and have written down. You should often **see** yourself accomplishing what you set out to accomplish. Imagine what it will feel like after all your hard work pays off. Creating this type of connection to your goal will help fuel you in your desire to attain what is necessary to make it (i.e., the goal) a reality.

"So, how do I write my goals? Where do I start?" you might ask. As much as your teammates, coaches, and parents want to help you, it ultimately lies on your shoulders to create your plan.

You might have already heard of "SMART" goals before. If not, it's an easy way to outline your goals as you are planning them out. The acronym stands for:

- **Specific**
- **Measurable**
- **Achievable**
- **Relevant**
- **Time-Limited**

You can make your SMART goals list based on the following:

SPECIFIC

All goals should be specific, and simple, and must get to the point. If you can't accurately tell what you *specifically* want, it will be hard to achieve it. Imagine going into a restaurant and telling the waiter, "I want food," without being specific about exactly what you want. If you don't know what you want, there's a greater chance that you'll end up with something you don't want. *So, **be specific!***

MEASURABLE

Are the goals you have something that you can measure? For example, writing down something like "I want to have a better attitude" is not measurable. Even though it's a great goal, it's not something you can count or represent with numbers. You can't prove it with facts that everyone can see or measure.

ACHIEVABLE

I'm sure you've heard the saying "anything is possible." That statement can be true for almost anything. But being *realistic* can help you stay focused. There is a difference between *being truthful to yourself and doubting yourself.* If you make a goal to hit two (2) home runs per game for the new baseball season and you've never hit one before in your life, is that an attainable, achievable goal? Probably not. What about if you make a goal to score 30 or more points in your next basketball game, but you've never even scored as many as 10 points in *one* game before; is that a reasonable goal to have? That would be a goal that is very unlikely to be reached. In these examples, it doesn't mean that your goal wouldn't someday be reached *after* plenty of hard work and dedication. So, your objective is to try to have achievable goals that you might be able to realistically *"stretch."* For example, if you averaged seven (7) points a game in basketball last year, your goal for this year might be to average 10 points per game. Your *"stretch"* goal might be twelve (12). The goal, pun intended, is to aim high but be realistic.

It's okay to adjust goals as you progress. For example, if you are a pitcher in baseball or softball and you currently throw 50 mph, and your goal is to eventually soon be able to throw 70 mph, it's okay to set a goal to hit 55 mph first. This speed doesn't mean you are placing your immediate goals too low. After hitting 55 mph, you may then adjust your objective to 60 mph and so on. Eventually, these small attainable goals can lead you to an increase in performance, helping you reach the higher overall goal.

"Goals"

RELEVANT

Your goals must be relevant to something that you want to accomplish. In other words, it has to match up with or be related to the ultimate result you want to see. An athlete who aims to get stronger before the upcoming season is a good example. Therefore, a goal that would involve them being able to lift a certain amount of weight would be considered *relevant*.

TIME-LIMITED

When you believe that you have all the time in the world to accomplish something, it provides less motivation for you to get things done in a reasonable timeframe. Making sure you keep yourself focused with a timeline of when you should have specific goals complete will help ensure that you are progressing. In addition, it can give you more structure. An example could be someone who wants to run within a particular time range on their 1-mile run. Their timeline could look like this:

Month # 1- run a mile in under 8 minutes.
Month # 2- run a mile in under 7 minutes and 30 seconds
Month # 3- run a mile in under 7 minutes

The above is just an example that fits the particular activity, in this case, cross country or track. However, you could also use this format and ideology for other sports. The key is to ensure that you have some form of progress built into your plan that is measured by time. By doing so, you have a means by which you can hold yourself accountable.

SUCCESSFUL PEOPLE COMMIT FIRST AND FIGURE OUT THE DETAILS LATER.

-GRANT CARDONE

Here is a chart to overview SMART goals:

SMART GOALS

SPECIFIC

›› What is my goal?

›› What do I need to do to achieve it?

›› What are the challenges to this goal?

MEASURABLE

›› How will I measure my progress?

›› How will I know when the goal is accomplished?

ACHIEVABLE

›› Is this a realistic goal for me at the moment?

RELEVANT

›› How does this goal make sense for what I want to accomplish?

›› Do I have everything I need to make my goal a reality?

TIME-BOUND

›› How much time will it take for me to complete my goal?

Writing down your goals will help you be able to go back and reflect on them so you can track your progress. After writing your goals down, read over them often. This re-reading will keep your goals fresh on your mind, which will make you think of new ways that you can go about achieving them.

Be excited about your goals, but do not *brag* about them to others before you achieve them. Being confident that you can accomplish what you want to do is different from being *arrogant* about it. Always strive to prove something to *yourself* before attempting to prove anything to others.

Constantly adjust your goals to your progress. As you advance in skill and meet your goals, find new goals for yourself to meet that are going to challenge you. It's important to take a deep breath and enjoy how far you have come when you *do* accomplish a goal that you have set.

Your strongest muscle and worst enemy is your mind. Train it well.

HOW VISUALIZATION CAN HELP IN AIDING GOAL SETTING

Visualization is a technique used by some of the world's most elite athletes. It's no different than daydreaming, except that it can be a lot more intentional with a focus on imagining a specific goal the athlete would like to accomplish. When someone daydreams, it may consist of a conversation they plan to have with someone later on, what they will eat for dinner, or something else dealing with everyday life. For athletes, this type of "daydreaming" may involve properly executing a play that the coach taught you and seeing yourself help the team win on a crucial play.

It's important not only to visualize your ultimate goals but also to see yourself successfully completing the smaller steps in between that will help you achieve the ultimate goals. For example, suppose you want to be a starter for the new team you just joined. Don't *only* envision being a starter but also see yourself working hard and having success in practice and doing the extra work outside of team practice that will help you get better and ultimately earn your coach's trust. Remember, it's vital to visualize the *in-between* steps so that you can stay on track with your goals and not get too overwhelmed by the overall vision.

THE POWER OF POSITIVE AFFIRMATIONS

Words are powerful. What are ideas and thoughts without words to express them? The words you choose to describe and relate to your athletic performance, believe it or not, can shape how you view yourself, ultimately impacting your overall athletic accomplishments. Confidence is very crucial, as you may already know. However, your confidence can derive from your words and thoughts about yourself and your circumstances.

A positive thought outweighs a negative one *dramatically* and opens you up to a positive possibility. Sometimes you cannot change your surroundings or circumstances, but you can change how you **think** and the words you use to describe them.

How we think and feel creates our state of being.

A person's mind is a mighty tool, consistently believing whatever it is told. We can feed our minds what we want to program it with, good or bad. If you look at many successful athletes today, they not only envision their success, they *expect* it. Because so many outside influences can negatively affect our confidence, we must do our part by being proactive with creating a positive mindset. We can do this by using *positive affirmations*.

An affirmation can be **anything you say or think about yourself**. Continually using *positive* affirmations can help to remove negative thoughts. When negative thinking about yourself comes into your mind, to prevent it from gaining any momentum, you can interrupt those negative thoughts by immediately using a **positive affirmation**.

Here are some examples of POSITIVE affirmations:

"I am going to have a great game today!"

"I am a great leader for my team."

"I love hard work because it makes me better."

"My coaches love my effort and attitude."

"My teammates respect me, and I encourage them to want to be better."

Question- "What if I don't fully believe in these affirmations I say about myself? I am not convinced that what I am saying in my affirmations about myself is possible or even true."

Answer- "The more you begin to write down or voice out loud what it is you want and the traits you would like to have as if you already have them, the quicker you may start to *believe* it's possible. You begin to gravitate towards more positivity overall by repeatedly continuing to have such positive thoughts."

YOU DON'T NEED SUCCESS TO FEEL EMPOWERED. FEEL EMPOWERED, AND IT WILL LEAD YOU TO SUCCESS.

- JOE DISPENZA

You may be wondering whether you should SAY or WRITE these affirmations down. You can do either. However, doing BOTH would help in supporting the outcomes you want to see.

BUILD GOOD HABITS AND CREATE MOMENTUM

Sometimes getting started can be the most challenging task in reaching a goal. Therefore, learning how to ride the wave of momentum is very crucial. After finding the motivation to get started, maintaining momentum will help you stay *consistent* with taking actions that will help you reach your goals.

Forming good habits starts with being **committed** to doing *something* to improve yourself, no matter how small it may seem. For example, there may be some days when you do not feel at your best or aren't motivated to go and train for your sport. You may be tired or have a desire to do something else with your time - but even on those days, if you gather up the strength to carve out a little bit of time to devote towards your mission to get better, it will build some confidence to keep you moving in the right direction.

A LITTLE BIT IS BETTER THAN NOTHING AT ALL when it comes to maintaining your momentum.

CHAPTER 7
MAKING EXCUSES

"IF IT'S IMPORTANT TO YOU, YOU WILL FIND A WAY. IF NOT, YOU WILL FIND AN EXCUSE."

Before blaming someone else for your lack of success, be sure you've removed all obstacles you've set up against yourself. Most of the time, an athlete will be the *real* one to blame for their failures but will often assign those reasons to someone or something else as if that someone or something else had control of *their* performance. Even if an athlete doesn't attribute their failures to others, they may still attempt to credit inanimate objects for their problems. For instance, they may blame the grass for being too wet during the game, the sun shining in their eyes that prevented them from seeing the ball, or any other reason for blaming something or someone. There may be difficult circumstances that you encounter from time to time, but there are distinct reasons why you should *not* use them as a crutch for why you might have fallen short of achieving your goal.

When you blame situations or others for your shortcomings, it takes power away from you to change your situation. Giving other people or circumstances the power to dictate how you perform will always leave you at the mercy of others and conditions out of your control. To be a top athlete, you must continually set your *performance standards* and do your best to stick to them. Regardless of what anyone else says or does, it should not penetrate your mindset and affect your level of play.

When you say things like:

"I can't score more points per game because almost every referee for our games makes bad calls."

You are shifting blame to a set of circumstances that are out of your control. Sure, for instance, in a sport like basketball, there are some referees out there who make bad calls. However, if this is your mindset in every game, you will spend less and less time focusing on doing what it takes to succeed and more and more time focusing on how someone else is going to prevent you from achieving. So, to be a supreme athlete, at *all* times, your mind has to be focused on being successful. If ever you fail in any way, your thoughts must be directed immediately into how you can turn that failure into success and perhaps use it as fuel for something positive. When you decide to take responsibility, you gain a whole new level of control. Feeling that you have more control over the outcome of your performance will give you a lot of confidence and reassurance as opposed to feeling anxiety from not knowing if or when others will cause your downfall.

IT'S OKAY THAT YOU'RE NOT PERFECT!

So why do people make excuses, whether to another person or, most importantly, to themselves? Many athletes believe that they need an explanation for being imperfect. Think about it for a minute. If you ponder this, you will see how distorted the average individual's mindset is regarding failure. Athletes believe that if they make a mistake, it *must* be immediately followed by a good reason for why it happened. In an attempt to not feel judged for making a mistake, many athletes think that they have to immediately make every potential judge of their performance, such as coaches or parents, aware of *why* they made a mistake. Perhaps it can make them feel better or less of a failure to explain themselves, which is understandable because no one wants to feel as if they aren't playing up to standard. Indeed, no one wants to feel as if they are less than others, and no one wants to feel embarrassed. Always remember that you are human and that every human on the planet makes mistakes. You are far from alone in your imperfections.

BE YOUR OWN TEAM WITHIN A TEAM

An athlete has to learn to be their own team and support system at times. Being your "own team within a team" requires you to be completely self-reliant *mentally*. Of course, when playing a team sport, you must rely on teammates to make things work. However, when it comes to your mental state, you must be self-reliant (not having to depend on others for you to think positively). It's always good to welcome encouragement from others for motivation, but it's another thing to *rely* on it. You have to be the type of player who will play their best game regardless of outside influence from others.

DON'T MAKE EXCUSES; MAKE ADJUSTMENTS

Another reason it's not a good idea to make excuses is that you will be far less likely to make the necessary adjustment(s) to avoid making the *same* mistake in the future. Going back to being in control of your performance, if someone else is the reason for your failure, why even adjust? Why go the extra mile to work hard to ensure it doesn't happen again? You might as well sit back and let things continue to happen the way they have been if that's the case. But remember, to be a superior-level athlete, you must act with your mind on the deliberate path of excellence.

TAKING RESPONSIBILITY

Responsibility is one of the most vital traits of a leader. Before someone can become a great leader for themselves (and eventually their team), they must understand the importance of being *responsible*. Excuses are the opposite of responsibility. When you take responsibility for where you are and how you perform, you automatically start freeing yourself from excuses. You will begin to take ownership of your *own* goals.

As mentioned, the personal power an athlete feels from being responsible for their situation can be boundless. It gives you a level of freedom you can't experience when you allow others around to dictate your level of success for you. However, with great power comes great responsibility. Having the freedom and choice of determining whether you fail or succeed can be intimidating for some. But, with no one to blame, you have the freedom to take action to improve your situation or sit around and wait for things to get better. Which will you choose?

Responsibility = The Ability to Respond

When you break down the word, you will see its true meaning. Having the ability to respond accordingly to the challenges of a superior athlete is what responsibility is all about.

- How do you **respond** when things don't go your way?
- Do you have the **ability** to be resilient and keep striving towards whatever goal you have?
- How do you **respond** when you do well?
- Do you have the **ability** to remain focused and hungry enough to keep pressing forward, or do you relax?

DON'T LET OTHERS MAKE EXCUSES FOR YOU

Many times, the family and friends of athletes that love them will make the most convenient excuses for the athletes to cheer them up, so they don't feel bad. Accepting the encouraging cheer when you have had a negative performance isn't bad, but *do not* allow yourself to buy into the excuses that others may lay out for you. Family, friends, and teammates can sometimes allow you to remain stuck being an average athlete because they feed you compliments during inopportune times, like giving a baby a pacifier to keep them from crying. It's a similar effect. Those close to you don't want to see you heartbroken, disappointed, or upset. Therefore, they aren't always the best ones to talk to when an athlete needs to hear the absolute *truth*. Hence, **finding a good coach or mentor to hold you accountable when needed is essential.**

Let others know that you do not expect to be babied or treated with sympathy. Athletes who react negatively to coaches when they get corrected or are asked to adjust run the risk of never being told when they are doing something wrong. Giving negative backlash to a coach will make coaches less likely to approach you with corrections you need to make in the future. Remember, not being coachable can often be an annoyance to a coach. Those who are less likely to be able to handle corrections from a coach when they are doing something wrong are more likely to continue the same mistakes.

Be the type of athlete that can take true, honest, genuine constructive criticism. Hearing the truth from a trusted coach will give you the keys to what you need to know to make corrections to your performance. Those who risk potentially leading you down the wrong path because they are afraid to tell you the truth about yourself cannot help you much. As an athlete intensely focused on your goals, you can still love and appreciate your close loved ones who offer you advice. Just know how to recognize those who tell you what you *need* to hear versus those who tell you what you *want* to hear.

You have the power in your hands to **change your mindset**, and when you do, it will **change your attitude**, which, in turn, will inspire you to **change your actions**. Those actions will eventually lead you to get different results. Changing your *mindset* is the very first step, though.

CHANGE YOUR MINDSET ➡ CHANGE YOUR ATTITUDE ➡ CHANGE YOUR ACTIONS

START WHERE YOU ARE

Instead of making excuses about where you are currently related to where you want to be, put your focus and energy into doing the best you can *right now*, with whatever resources and access you have currently available. Valuable time can be wasted focusing on what you don't have.

This could be things like:

- The equipment you are not able to afford.
- The team or coach for whom you wish you played.
- The practice field that you think could look better.

If you don't have the resources, access to training, or specific equipment, flip the situation to your advantage. Something like this could help propel you to new heights because you may be forced to get creative with new ways of improving yourself. See it as an opportunity to make yourself tougher than those who may have had things handed to them a little easier.

A prime example would be young baseball players in the Dominican Republic, a small island in the Caribbean. Here is where many current Major League Baseball superstars are born and raised. The passion for the sport is so great that many Major League teams have academies in the Dominican Republic, where they house young prospects who have the potential of one day being good enough to move to the United States and play for a major league team.

With many parts of the country being poor, kids find anything they can to practice the game. Often they use bottle caps to serve as baseballs and find broomsticks to use as baseball bats. With some barely having shoes on their feet and folded cardboard as a substitute for a glove, they still manage to find a way to work on their game. *They do as best they can with what they have.* After taking a trip and witnessing it for myself, I found it astounding that kids were playing in flip-flops in the street. The entire time I saw very few excuses being made. The main reason for this may have been because they have seen others come from the same situation and still find a way to make it.

ADVERSITY BUILDS CHARACTER

One crucial thing a strong-minded athlete must realize is that when they face adversity, it doesn't give them the green light to make excuses for their failure. Adverse situations can come in numerous forms and types for an athlete. These difficulties could be physical, mental, emotional, or social. Some might include:

Physical - *injuries, height or weight disadvantage, skill or natural ability (i.e., speed)*
Mental - *nervousness, anxiety,*
Emotional - *feeling down about failing, anger about performance,*
Social - *negative interactions with other teammates or coaches*

These are some of the four main types of adversity that an athlete may experience. You may have experienced all forms, or perhaps just a couple. Regardless, one of these forms may appear at some point in your athletic career. If it does, know that it can be overcome and that you're not the first to go through it. One of the biggest reasons that people find it hard to go through adversity is because they feel like their situation is unique. It is, in a way, but not how most people figure. They are often unaware of stories about those who dealt with precisely what they have dealt with, not just dealt with it, but have overcome it. Learning the stories of other athletes who have overcome more significant challenges than you is another way to help reframe your situation. It can show us that not only did someone overcome similar adversity, but that someone was able to overcome even more incredible adversity, which ultimately helps us realize that we can overcome our lesser challenges.

Remember, you are human. Making mistakes is a part of the process. If you ever find yourself making excuses for your results, let it serve as a wake-up call to take your power back.

"EVERY PERSON ON THE PLANET HAS A DISABILITY – NOT JUST THOSE WE CAN SEE. AND WE ALL CHOOSE WHETHER WE ALLOW OUR LIVES TO BE DEFINED BY THEM OR NOT."
– KYLE MAYNARD

The story of Kyle Maynard is an extraordinary one that is a perfect example of studying those who have overcome. Kyle has spent a lifetime overcoming significant adversities. His hardships were more of a physical nature, often leading to mental, emotional, and social difficulties, which it most definitely did for him. Kyle joined the wrestling team in the 6th grade. What's interesting is that Kyle lost his first 35 matches. Even more interesting is that he continued to wrestle in many events while steadily taking losses. What's even *more* interesting than that is that Kyle was born with no arms and legs. He had no limbs from his elbows and his knees down.

He never quit and continued to work very hard at his new sport. By the time he entered high school, his talents had started to be noticed. He had found ways to turn  his condition into an advantage and a disadvantage to his opponents. He went on to win 36 matches his senior year and placed 12th in the 103-pound weight class. As a result, he was honored by the National Wrestling Hall of Fame as an inductee.

To learn more about Kyle's story, check out his book "No Excuses."

CHAPTER 8

BECOMING A LEADER, TAKING OWNERSHIP & ACCOUNTABILITY

HOW TO BE A LEADER ON YOUR TEAM

Many think leaders are born. While some may indeed be born with innate *characteristics* that would make them a more *likely* leader, if the statement were true, then it would mean if you're not a leader right now, you can *never* be one. Since being labeled a "leader" is based on the *person's actions*, it's possible for those who don't carry the traits of a leader to *change* their actions and *become* one. So, in actuality, you don't have to be "born a leader" to change your actions and start *acting* like a leader through your words, thoughts, and behaviors.

People worldwide admire leaders because they are known for giving their best effort every time, and they represent what it means to help others in achieving goals and encouraging others when they make mistakes. This ability to lead is why everyone wants a leader on their team. And leaders have different styles. Some may be more vocal and have a lot to say, thus ensuring everyone knows what's going on during practice or games. On the other hand, some leaders will take more silent and subtle actions, like leading the team during pregame stretches or being first in line for drills at practice. Someone who leads by *example*, and not just with their words, can *also* be an effective leader.

As a leader, you should <u>never</u> expect your teammates to do something that <u>YOU</u> are also not willing to do!

"WHAT IF I'M SHY? CAN I STILL BE A LEADER?"

Any athlete can learn to become more of a leader on their team. Some might think they have to be "loud" on the field to lead a team effectively. Even though some athletes are well-suited to be vocal leaders based on their particular personalities, you don't *have* to be extra vocal if that leadership style doesn't fit who *you* are. Leadership consists of more than being verbal; it consists of your attitude, mental toughness, ways you encourage others, and, more importantly - your actions. Would a louder and more vocal player than the average teammate be a good leader if they had a *terrible* attitude, complained about practice each time, and talked badly about the other teammates? Absolutely not! Being *louder* than your teammates doesn't always equate to being a *good* leader.

Leaders rarely make excuses, and they quickly take responsibility for their mistakes **without blaming anyone else**. Athletes who always whine, complain, or blame others for their mistakes can never be fully respected as a leader on the team. Respect is one of the common byproducts of good leadership. Leaders **earn** respect from their teammates and coaches.

LEADERS VS. NON-LEADERS

What separates *those who lead* effectively and *those who don't* is the difference in their **decision-making**. The difference between the two is highlighted by the fact that one makes better decisions. When you make decisions, you are more in control. When you don't make good, firm decisions, things happen *to* you and not *for* you. So, when you are solid and determined to make a decision for your betterment, things start to happen *for* you.

> **Are you going to let things happen <u>TO</u> you or <u>FOR</u> you?**
> **Are you going to <u>LET</u> things happen or <u>MAKE</u> things happen?**

Most who aren't leaders want the comfort of knowing that someone else will make all of the decisions for them in areas such as when to practice and work on getting better in their own time, what to eat before a game, when to congratulate a teammate on something positive, etc.

When you lack decision-making skills, your teammates will sense it, and it will be harder for them to see you as a leader. Giving one's respect to a leader starts with **trust**. Your teammates will follow your lead if they trust you! People can tell if you're hesitant and unsure of yourself. Unsure athletes are uncertain of themselves because they know they haven't put in the necessary work to be qualified to lead others.

No player can lead their teammates without first proving that they are in charge of *themselves*. Through your personal choices, you will influence others. Making sure that you don't fall victim to the peer pressure of being *average* is very important. Always set a standard of excellence for *yourself* that can't be broken by others who decide that they want to be less than what they are capable of being.

By becoming a leader, you eliminate the chances of being led by the wrong people. And as the old saying goes, "if you want to guarantee something is done right, you have to do it yourself." That includes leading **yourself** first.

You should be prepared to lead your team in *every* situation (game or practice), not just when you *"feel like it."* Taking on the challenge of leading a team but only doing it when you *feel* like it won't cut it. If you went about it that way, this would mean that you could only lead *sometimes*, and that is *not* what leaders do. Being a good leader for your team has to be a part of who you are *all the time*. Being a leader on any team comes with significant responsibilities that only a few can handle. Those who choose to be leaders *must* have **self-discipline**. Without discipline, it will be hard to stick to the behavior of true leaders.

Choosing to become a leader requires discipline because *others* are now counting on you. When you know that others count on you, you don't want to let them down. This accountability is all about stepping up your game for a more significant cause than yourself. The idea of others counting on you doesn't mean that you need to get down on yourself if you make a mistake.

Leaders are still human. They make mistakes. However, they know they are responsible for going about their mistakes differently because everyone is looking up to them.

5 THINGS THAT ALL LEADERS DO

1. Take responsibility for their mistakes

Taking ownership of your mistakes shows integrity. Teammates and coaches can trust players like this. Moreover, those who take responsibility are usually more likely to correct their errors than those who tend to blame others. After all, "blamers" don't believe that the situation had anything to do with them from the beginning.

2. Never give up

Having perseverance is very important. No one wants to be led by a person who gives up when things get tough. And like those who take responsibility, teammates are more likely to trust those who never give up. There is a certain level of integrity you need to stick with it and complete the task, whatever it may be. Those who demonstrate this trait will continue to gain the respect of those around them.

3. Reframe "problems" as "opportunities"

Attitude is the difference between seeing something as a problem versus seeing it as an **opportunity** (or even a challenge). Always see your more difficult moments as opportunities to overcome and *grow* as a person. Challenges are designed to test your character, just like quizzes and tests in school are designed to test your knowledge. Anytime there is an obstacle in your way, this creates an opportunity to prove something to **yourself**.

4. Instill confidence in others by staying positive

A leader is someone who may see a teammate having a difficult time or that has made a mistake and goes to them to pick them up and let them know that everything will be alright. This kind of teammate is someone that can build trust within the team. It will also make your relationship with teammates a lot stronger. Helping to boost a teammate's spirits during tough times will benefit the entire team and is something your teammate will never forget.

5. They show <u>confidence</u>, not arrogance

A leader's self-confidence rubs off on teammates and helps them raise their level of performance. Many teammates thrive off of the confident behavior of those around them. If an athlete isn't feeling as optimistic as they should, they may need some help from elsewhere. This optimism is almost as if they *borrow* confidence from someone else until they have enough to sustain themselves.

Arrogance is not a good trait if you want to gain respect as a leader. An arrogant (sometimes known as "cocky") athlete feels they are more significant than other teammates or opponents. However, having self-confidence and belief in yourself does not have to equate to feeling superior or more *important* than anyone else.

Becoming a team leader takes a special type of athlete. It doesn't require you to be born with leadership skills to be good at it. It's something that you can work on simply by knowing what comprises a leader. Anyone who dedicates themselves to following the key elements of leadership can earn the respect of their teammates as a leader. Leading with your words is an integral part, but leadership through your actions and words will go even further.

BE OF VALUE TO YOUR TEAM

"A team is only as strong as its weakest link."

Being a liability to your team would mean that you are the cause for your squad failing in one way or another. Of course, all athletes fail from time to time, but to be considered an actual liability to your team would mean that you are *consistently* doing things within your control that could be harmful to the team's success.

Here is a small list of things that might cause you to be a liability to your team:

1. Not knowing the team's strategies or plays.

2. Complaining and spreading negativity among the group.

3. Putting down other teammates by talking negatively about them.

4. Not playing hard or not trying your very best during games or practice.

When you commit to a team, you should strive to uphold the responsibility of being on that team. Keep in mind that even if you decide that the sport you play isn't a true long-term passion for you, you are on a team that could have others who are deeply invested and truly care. For this reason, you should be sure to give all you have out of respect for those you play alongside.

Being a liability would mean that the team has a greater chance of failing to reach their goals due to a habit or tendency you are exhibiting. You cannot be both good and bad for your team. You can only be one or the other. So, how do you avoid being a liability? It's simple – strive to be the *opposite* characteristics of what is described in the list above for teammates that are liabilities.

1. Be sure to fully know all aspects of the team's strategies and plays. For instance, if you play a team sport, know what your job is and where you need to be during every situation of a game.

2. Speak positively about your team and coaches. Use positive speech at practice and games.

3. When speaking to teammates, only say things that are positive and uplifting.

4. Always give the very best performance effort possible. Only *you* can know just how hard you are trying. Don't cheat yourself.

It is also a contradiction to be both a bad influence on your team *and* a team leader.

NO ONE OWES YOU ANYTHING

Athletes need to get away from the notion that coaches, parents, or teammates owe them things they want. This belief could be in the form of praise, trophies, a pat on the back, or a particular position on the field. However, this is not to say that coaches and parents should do their jobs to help you in your efforts. It's to say that you shouldn't rely on it to determine whether you will give your all.

Of course, if you receive significant help from coaches, teammates, and parents, all the better. But it isn't something you should seek or let worry you.

Athletes often feel like their coaches owe them the playing time they want. They think that their teammates owe them the respect of a leader. They may believe that their parents owe them a certain level of support. While you may hope that you get all of these things, what if you don't?

What if your parent(s) don't support your goals? Will you give up on them?

What if your coaches don't see you as capable of playing a particular position on the team? Will you stop trying to prove your capabilities to them?

What if your teammates don't see you as the leader you aspire to be? Will you then stop doing your best to lead your team?

Never ask for anyone to give you the respect you feel you deserve as an athlete. Instead, it would be best if you always carried yourself in a fashion that will have you *earn* the respect of others, including your parents, coaches, and teammates. Trying to force people to give you a certain level of regard, admiration, or attention that you did not earn will only have them give you a false sense of the respect that you seek.

PLAYING TIME

How often you play on your team or what position is usually determined by the coach. However, it's best to tell yourself that no one else determines what you get but you. If you have this mindset, you will be forced to make no excuses about where you end up on your path, so go out there and prove your worth on the team. A champion athlete shouldn't want it to be easy or handed to them. Obtaining your role on the team through your hard work and effort feels much more satisfying.

Be so good that they can't ignore you.

If you are experiencing a lack of playing time, overall, or in a particular position, first look at what you can do to change that. Don't look to blame others or make excuses because that is less likely to help you. It may lead to feeling sorry for yourself, and no person has *ever* empowered themselves when doing so. Feeling sorry for oneself will make a person less likely to take action because there is nothing more that people who feel sorry for themselves want than to have others feel sorry for them and reinforce their victimhood.

When you hope for anyone to hand you something you should have earned through your actions, you give *them* the power to decide your feelings. How you feel determines your thoughts. Your thoughts dictate your behaviors. So allowing your emotions to be swayed by others could equate to having less control of your destiny. Don't allow others to determine how hard you work. Whether someone else acknowledges your hard work, positive attitude, or skill should be irrelevant to you. Yes, it feels good to be recognized. Of course, receiving compliments is fun and acceptable at times, but don't allow it to enter your mind and be a reason not to continue pressing forward. Always remember that you are doing your best for yourself first and foremost.

"THE ONLY PERSON WHO CAN STOP YOU FROM REACHING YOUR GOALS IS YOU."

—JACKIE JOYNER-KERSEE

EXPECT THINGS TO BE TOUGH

There are plenty of things you should expect on your journey. Your expectations set the tone. One major factor that keeps athletes from working hard is that working hard is *tough*. The obstacles to working hard are more mental than physical. When going through training for your sport, whether it be drills, running, or weight lifting, you will encounter some struggles and may even feel like quitting. These times can be overwhelming mentally and emotionally. However, if you go into the situation knowing that things may get tough for you, you will be less likely to be overwhelmed when "the going gets tough."

CHAPTER 9

TAKING CARE OF YOUR BODY

Taking Care of Your Body is one of the most important chapters of this book. No matter how incredibly skilled you are as an athlete, it will mean _nothing_ if you aren't physically able to compete, whether due to an injury or to your body not being in good enough condition to play at a high level. Likewise, you can't make an impact on your team unless you are _able to physically play._ With that being said, it's vitally important that you take care of your body as best you can.

Athletes who don't pay attention to or take good care of their bodies will oftentimes compromise their performance at one point or another. Not being fully healthy can make it difficult to play and help your team to the best of your ability. Your skill means *nothing* if you aren't able to compete in team competition when it really counts.

How you TRAIN, EAT, and SLEEP is super important!

Following are three (3) major elements in particular that are important to your health as an athlete:

1. **Getting Your Body Prepared for Practices and Games**

   It's super important that you be sure your total body is warmed up *and* properly stretched out before games and practices to ensure that you don't injure any muscles or joints. Some injuries aren't as easily preventable, but warmups and stretching will give you the opportunity to prevent an injury *before* it happens. Not only is it key to do these things to avoid injuries, but it's also key to performing at your highest level. It will help give you the ability to run as fast and be as quick as you need to be.

   Most athletes are not serious about taking care of their bodies, which is why doing so can give *you* a tremendous opportunity to get an edge over your competition. Properly preparing your body is just as much mental as it is physical. Knowing that you have done the extra work preparing this way will give you more confidence that you are *ready* to go.

Great athletes find ways to focus on the little things others don't take the time to. So, players need to warm up and stretch for practices with the *same* intensity as if they were playing a real game. Warming up and stretching is how you prepare your mind to be ready on game day because your body is used to the routine of being *geared up* for intense movement.

Besides warmups immediately before a game or practice, what you do to train your body regularly is critical, especially as athletes get older. In terms of regular training, before high school, it's recommended that athletes do not participate in heavy weight lifting. However, pushups, sit-ups, and running for conditioning can create a bit of an edge for the younger age groups.

2. What You Eat and Drink

A crucial factor to consider is eating more foods that will strengthen your body as an athlete. These will include items that do not weigh you down or cause you to get tired and sleepy after you consume them. Greasy fast foods, heavy meats & unhealthy snacks that are high in sugar are all things that you should avoid before competition and practices. It's important to know that foods that take a long time to digest (i.e., that are heavy) cause your body to use lots of energy during the process. So, as more of the body's energy is used for the digestive system, less blood and oxygen are available for the rest of your brain and muscles to use while you compete. This event is why people often get sleepy or tired after eating a heavy meal. We can all relate to this at some point.

Before a competition, you should always seek to eat foods that are high in nutrition and easy for your body to digest. These foods include light fruits such as apples, bananas, pineapples, and plenty of other types that will help give you a quick energy source and won't weigh you down. Hydrating with water is also very important. Since your body releases a lot of fluids when you play, it's vital to replenish so your body can operate at its highest level. Water is essential to how the body functions overall. It's no secret why drinking plenty of water is vital for athletes. So don't wait until you are thirsty before you start to drink water. Even if you are not thirsty at the moment, it will be good for you to drink water to prevent dehydration *before* it happens. The body can experience dehydration if it doesn't get enough fluids. It can cause an athlete many problems and is more likely to occur in weather where the temperatures are high. Making sure you are hydrated hours before can prevent this.

Here are some signs that you may be dehydrated:

- **Thirst**
- **Sticky or dry mouth**
- **Headache**
- **Dark colored urine**
- **Muscle cramps**

Be very careful with sports drinks you consume that have various flavors. Many sports drinks on the market contain loads and loads of sugar to make them taste sweeter and more enjoyable. Even though it may be tempting, avoid drinking too much of any sports drink with high sugar content.

"A DIET THAT IS BAD FOR YOUR OVERALL HEALTH CAN'T BE GOOD FOR YOUR PERFORMANCE."

-KOBE BRYANT

3. Sleep

Sleep is a super important factor for the average person, let alone for an athlete. If a lack of sleep or improper sleep can impact someone doing normal daily activities, how do you think it affects an athlete attempting to perform at their highest level?

Most athletes focus mainly on their training and some on their diet. Advanced athletes focus on both. Elite athletes ensure they train at a high level, eat well, *and* get quality rest. *Quality* rest is the key.

Some experts say that sleeping habits are even more important than diet. Think of sleep as recharging the body -- similar to what you do with a cellphone or tablet. A cellphone, laptop, or electrical device that we use in our day-to-day life wouldn't be able to function at full power without successfully recharging. Some studies have revealed that a lack of sleep increases the likelihood of athletes having injuries and that a proper amount of rest can help athletes recover faster. This recovery process means they will experience less soreness after training and will be ready to play at a high level in a quicker time frame post-competition/practice.

To ensure more quality sleep, be sure to:

Avoid sleeping with light. Sleep in a dark room. Turn all lights in the room *off*. Looking at a cellphone, tablet, or television screen before falling asleep can significantly affect sleep since it produces artificial light that can trick the body into thinking it's daytime, which will throw off the body's natural sleep cycle.

Avoid sleeping with noise - Sleep in a quiet room. Noise will engage the mind and cause it to process sounds and information it hears, thus preventing it from attaining the complete rest it needs while sleeping.

*Ultimately, this is why it is best to turn the television OFF when it's time to sleep. Both noise and light could prevent the body from entering the deep sleep necessary for optimal recovery.

Avoid eating before bed - your heart rate increases during digestion, so it's best not to go to bed right after eating a meal.

Avoid drinks with caffeine - caffeinated beverages cause adrenaline production to increase, which will do the _opposite_ in helping your body to be calm and relaxed before sleep.

Doing the above can help athletes develop good sleeping habits, which can pay off in the long run.

HOW MANY HOURS OF SLEEP SHOULD AN ATHLETE GET PER NIGHT?

Experts suggest getting 8 or 9 hours of sleep as a good range to aim for when possible.

Not getting enough sleep could result in the following:

- Lack of concentration and focus
- Decreased endurance (getting tired more quickly)
- Poor decision making
- Increased chance of injury

"PROPER SLEEP HAS HELPED ME GET TO WHERE I AM TODAY AS AN ATHLETE AND IT'S SOMETHING THAT I WILL CONTINUE TO RELY ON EVERY DAY."

–TOM BRADY

DEALING WITH INJURIES

If you play any sport long enough, injuries are always possible. Some injuries happen gradually over time, while others occur in an instant. Instant injuries are called "acute injuries." Some injuries are more preventable than others, but what happens when you do all you can to prevent them and still suffer an acute injury? An example of an acute injury would be a twisted ankle or a broken bone caused by a fall or collision with an opponent. We all know that injuries are no fun. They can hurt as well as cause emotional stress. You may feel like you have let your team and/or family down when you get injured.

As an athlete, you should never lie about *not* being injured when you are because you're afraid of what others will think or say. The pressure to perform and please the team, coaches, and your parents can be tremendous. That is natural. However, plenty of athletes were truly injured but failed to tell a parent or coach and ended up prolonging the injury or making it worse. Some injuries can get worse if you do not tend to them immediately. This delay will only compound the issue and cause even more frustration. Which would you prefer, missing a game or two or half (or all) of an entire season of play?

Listen to your body. Don't ignore unusual pains.

Pay very close attention to what you feel with your body. If you are unsure what to do to feel better, be sure to see a doctor or specialist for help.

Here are some things to remember as it relates to injury:

1. **It's not your fault** - injuries happen to most athletes at one time or another. Some of the best athletes in the world deal with acute and gradual injuries that last for short periods and lengthier ones. An injury does not define who you are. The only thing within your control is remaining confident that you can do what needs to be done to return to playing.

2. **Things will get better** - when an injury happens, it can seem like it will last forever. The frustration and the anxiety that may come with it can create a lot of uncertainty. Remember that your body can and will heal. Stay positive and take the proper measures from doctors or coaches to recover from your injury as quickly as possible. Put your focus on coming back better and stronger than you were before.

3. **Don't let the fear of injury steal your joy** - anyone who's experienced an injury before and returned to playing understands that it may continue to linger in the back of your mind, even

after you've fully recovered. Do your best in rehabbing during your healing time, and don't allow yourself to worry about the rest.

"I HATED EVERY MINUTE OF TRAINING, BUT I SAID, DON'T QUIT, SUFFER NOW AND LIVE THE REST OF YOUR LIFE AS A CHAMPION."

—MUHAMMAD ALI

CHAPTER 10
COMPETING WITHOUT FEAR

IF YOU ARE UNWILLING TO BE IN CONTROL OF YOUR MIND, SOMETHING OR SOMEONE ELSE WILL.

Fear is possibly the number 1 reason why some athletes can't perform at their highest level. Fear can kill an athlete's confidence, and without a doubt, it is confidence's biggest enemy. Since the two can't occupy an athlete's mind simultaneously, the athlete needs to pick a side. If you want to be the best you can be, you will choose *confidence* and leave the fear behind. So, how do you do this?

First, you should understand the difference between playing *fearlessly* and playing *recklessly*. When an athlete plays fearlessly, it means they are playing with more confidence in themselves and a stronger belief that they will do well. When an athlete is playing recklessly, they may be playing *hard* and have some confidence, but ultimately they are playing with a lack of discipline that can harm the team's cause.

Many athletes may never become who they are capable of being because they are **letting fear stand in the way**. Awareness of your thoughts and how you use them is essential to managing fear. Let's be clear when discussing fear in this context; we aren't discussing being afraid that you will be harmed during gameplay or that something tragic will happen to you while playing. The fears that we speak of in this context are about the thoughts of:

- Making in-game mistakes and feeling embarrassed
- Getting yelled at by the coach
- Repeating mistakes from the past
- Not making your parents proud
- Playing against players that you feel are better than you
- Feeling nervous during a close game

Fears like these come from constant **negative thinking**.

Believe it or not, some athletes fear reaching their potential because it's an unfamiliar place for them. What does this mean, exactly? It's human nature to get used to certain things in our lives. When we *know* what to expect in situations, we feel at ease. There's a particular pattern or routine that we can trust. When it comes to whether we are a starter for our team or not, what position we play, or how our team relates to us, it's tempting to *stay* on that track simply because we *know* what to expect already. However, an athlete could feel unsure about what it's like "on the other side."

On the other side - where you are playing your best, having the best attitude, and being seen as a leader. Of course, everybody wants it, but very few are willing to face the fear that stands in the way of getting to "the other side."

STAY PRESENT

Your thoughts can be clouded by many things that don't need your immediate attention. In other words, you may neglect to think about the task at hand because you're busy thinking about something that *happened* (in the **past**) or that *hasn't happened* (in the **future**). Often, athletes with the least amount of focus are the ones who cannot remain in *the present* and *staying in the present* means thinking about each moment one by one as they come.

Presence isn't maintained by thinking about how the referee or umpire cheated you on a play earlier in the game. It's essential to focus on the very next play. All action that happens in sports happens in the present moment. Those who stay in the moment have a better chance of concentrating during gameplay and being more productive athletes. You can't correct a mistake that has already happened, and you can't accomplish something in the future that hasn't gotten here yet. Taking it "one play at a time" can relieve you from considerable worry and stress.

"WIN EACH PLAY"

So, being present means focusing, thinking, reacting, and competing at the moment that's happening right then and there. If you're thinking about what happened in your last game or what will happen in next week's game, you're not in the present *right now* in your current game. Always remember - since you can't control anything that has happened in the past and you can't do anything to help the future that is not yet here, it's best to focus all your energy on the *now*.

No matter what sport you compete in, all action happens in intervals. In baseball, the game moves one pitch at a time. In football, the game advances by each play after the teams huddle up to discuss the next play. In basketball, it happens per possession. Other sports operate similarly. So, what's the main point? Sports all have a stop-and-go period. The key to being present is concentrating to the best of your ability during the "go periods." During the "stop period," is when it's reasonable to perhaps reflect on a past situation that happened for you to figure out what needs to be done on the next, immediate play.

There is a difference between reflecting on things you've done to improve versus sulking in the past. If thinking about something in the past doesn't empower you, drop it from your mind. An excellent way to be *present* is to have a "Win this play" mindset. Since a lot of fears come from thinking too far into the future or thinking too much about the past, focus on playing the game from play to play. In your mind, every play should have a life of its own. No matter what position you are assigned on your team, no matter what the score is, play every play to the very best of your ability. Do it free of anything that has happened prior.

PLAY FREE
PLAY FAST
PLAY CONFIDENTLY

FEAR OF WHAT PARENTS WILL THINK

There may be no one whom you would rather impress than your parents. There is nothing to be ashamed of when it comes to this. It's natural for all people to want to live up to the greatness that their parents expect of them. Sometimes, however, this pressure can make athletes afraid to fail because they feel like their parents will think negatively of them. Has a parent ever affected your thinking to the point where it made you nervous or afraid to make mistakes? Many athletes may go through this during their careers. So, it takes a lot of mental toughness to overcome this *fear of failure* scenario because many athletes don't know how to deal with it.

It's not as easy as saying to yourself, "Just get over it," when your parents have negative things to say about your performance or if you feel like they aren't helping you think positively about yourself. Ultimately, your parents want to see you succeed. Unfortunately, some want so badly to see their athlete succeed that it may cause them to become overly passionate about their athlete's performances.

If you are ever going through something like this, it's important to be self-reliant mentally. It not only applies to parents but to others in general. This self-reliance means that you don't let how others see you in *their* mind affect how *you* play. To become the elite athlete you want to be, try to view all challenges as an opportunity to grow.

FEAR OF WHAT OTHER PEOPLE ARE THINKING ABOUT YOU

If an athlete lets others' perception of them be a determining factor in how they will play, they will always be at a disadvantage. Since someone's ideas about you can change as frequently as the weather, it's not a good idea to rely on how other people see you at any moment in time.

People generally tend to believe that others are pondering on their mistakes as much as they are. For example, let's say that you played a basketball game where you missed a crucial free throw that could have helped your team win at the end of the game. You may feel terrible because you believe your missed free throw was the main cause of your team's loss. Because of this, you may sulk on the way home, replaying it in your mind. Thinking of all the possible outcomes that could have happened. You may ask yourself, "Why did it have to be *me* that missed the free throw that caused our team to lose?" However, your teammate may be thinking about how they missed a free throw at the beginning of the game that would have altered the outcome, or another teammate might think about how they should have played better defense to stop the other team.

Each player is more than likely concerned with how everyone is judging them for what happened when in reality, each is too focused on what *they* did to focus their thoughts on what *other* teammates did. So, while many athletes will beat themselves up (in their mind) about something negative that they did, no one else is paying as much attention to it. Remembering this will help lessen the anxiety.

BE HONEST ABOUT ANY FEARS YOU MAY HAVE

Playing without fear doesn't mean that you shouldn't acknowledge them when you *do* have them. But, unfortunately, pretending your worries aren't there may cause you not to want to address them, which brings us to another fear. That is the fear of addressing a fear. It's a fear within a fear.

How do you have a fear of fear?

People are afraid to take a good, hard look at what makes them scared. The real fear comes from believing that if the thing that you fear happens, you won't be able to handle it emotionally, physically, or mentally.

Just remember, you've made mistakes before and have survived. Always focus on the next opportunity to succeed and perform well. Focus on the next play!

SUMMARY

- There will be challenges along the way. You should always expect that times may get tough at some point.
- Challenges make victories even sweeter.
- Instead of seeing mistakes as failures, see them as *opportunities*.
- Sports can teach people transferable, relatable skills that can assist you in life, not just sports.
- Fall in love with the **process** of becoming a better you, not just the outcome.
- Don't rely on talent alone on your journey.
- It's not what happens; it's how you **think** about what happens.

- See practice as "time *invested*," not simply "time *spent*."
- Prepare for practice with the same intensity that you would for a game (physically and mentally). This preparation helps to eliminate nervousness during competition when it counts the most.
- Always arrive to practice with clear goals in mind.
- Do not allow discomfort to discourage or intimidate you. **Embrace the discomfort** and it will help you grow stronger mentally.
- Focus on your weaknesses and not only your strengths.
- Welcome the idea of coaches critiquing you so you can know where you need to improve. Do not take their criticism personally.
- High-level athletes find ways to get **extra** practice outside of team practice.
- Finding a way to practice, even when you don't feel like it, can also be an excellent way to exercise your **willpower** "muscles."

- Managing emotions effectively is key to handling mistakes.
- Don't allow mistakes to distract you from doing your best in the next play.
- Reflect and learn from your past mistakes, but do not dwell on them.
- Things to NOT do when you don't get your way:
  - Get angry
  - Gossip
  - Develop a false sense of privilege
  - Give up
- Learn to appreciate what moments of failure can do for you.
- Things you **SHOULD** do when you don't get your way:
  - Ask (the coach) for clarification if you are unclear about something.
  - Turn inward - ask **yourself** what you think **you** could do better.
  - Set a goal - use goals to help you create a plan to improve.
- Playing time
  - Always take responsibility for what you can do to earn more playing time. Don't waste energy blaming others or making excuses.
  - Don't feel sorry for yourself.

- Each coach you have will be different in style, personality, character, and the amount of knowledge they have in the sport they are coaching.
- Never let your emotions stand in the way of your improvement. If you get so emotional about a coach that you miss out on how they can help you get better and improve, **you** are the one who loses.
- Don't solely rely on a coach to make you feel motivated to be your best. That should come from **you**. Instead, strive to be your best self, regardless of who your coach is.
- Learn as much as you can from <u>every</u> coach you encounter.
- Coaches do not like excuses from athletes.
- A coach yelling at you doesn't automatically mean they do not *like* you. Do not take criticism from a coach personally.
- If you are unsure about something a coach explains, **ask questions**.

CHAPTER 5: TAKING YOUR GAME TO THE NEXT LEVEL

- Being in a "comfort zone" can hold you back. View discomfort as a wake-up call.
- Fear of failing is a major reason many athletes don't attempt to improve themselves.
- Discipline is doing what needs to be done, even if you don't feel like doing it.
- Procrastination is a silent killer. Discipline can help prevent this unproductive habit.
- Although it's natural to compare yourself to others, it can negatively impact an athlete's mindset if it isn't put into a proper perspective.
- It's okay to look at others and see what pieces of their skillset you could borrow and use in your own game. Study athletes that are more advanced than you. Their success provides clues.

- *"A goal without a plan is just a wish."*
  - Antoine de Saint-Exupéry
- Self-improvement doesn't happen by accident. Writing down goals and taking action to reach them is the best way to reach new heights.
- Make your goals personalized and specific to you.
- You can use the **SMART** goals acronym to help you get started with writing out your goals. You can use it as a guideline:
  - **S-** Specific
  - **M-** Measurable
  - **A-** Achievable
  - **R-** Relevant
  - **T-** Time-Limited
- Practicing visualization can be used to help achieve your goals. However, don't just visualize your ultimate goals; also see yourself successfully completing the smaller steps in between that will help you achieve the ultimate goals.
- The **words** you choose to describe and relate to your athletic performance can shape how you view yourself, ultimately impacting your overall performance.
- Successful athletes **expect** success.
- When negative thinking about yourself comes into your mind, to prevent it from gaining any momentum, you can interrupt those negative thoughts by immediately using a *positive affirmation*.

CHAPTER 7: MAKING EXCUSES

- Always look within before attempting to blame others for your performance. Do not make excuses; *make adjustments!*
- When you blame situations, circumstances, or other people for your shortcomings, it takes your power away from being able to change your conditions.
- To be a supreme athlete, focus your mind on being successful. Always think of how you can turn failure into success.
- Taking personal responsibility gives you more control.
- It's okay not to be perfect. No one is. You are human; you will make mistakes.
- You have to learn how to be your own support system at times. Doing so requires being mentally self-reliant.
- *Responsibility = Ability to Respond*
- Don't allow others to make excuses for you (friends or family).
- Having a coach or mentor that will hold you *accountable* is needed.
- You have the power to **change your mindset**, which will **change your attitude** and inspire you to **change your actions**.
- Start where you are, with whatever resources you have. Not having resources may cause you to be more creative with figuring out ways to improve yourself.

- As a leader, you should *never* expect your teammates to do something *you* aren't willing to do!
- Leaders earn respect from their teammates and coaches.
- Good decision-making is a significant part of being a leader.
- Teammates are more likely to respect the leadership of a teammate they *trust*.
- Strive to be in charge of *yourself* before leading others.
- True leaders must have *self-discipline*.
- 5 Things that all good leaders do:
  o They take responsibility for their mistakes.
  o They never give up.
  o They reframe "problems" as "*opportunities*."
  o They instill confidence in others by staying positive.
  o They show *confidence*, not arrogance.
- When it comes to playing time, champion athletes do not want it handed to them. Instead, they obtain their role on the team through hard work and effort, which feels much more satisfying.
- Expect the journey to be tough, but challenge yourself to be *tougher!*

CHAPTER 9: TAKING CARE OF YOUR BODY

- As an athlete, you must take care of your body no matter how talented you may be.
- How you train, eat, and sleep is vital to your overall health as an athlete.
- Getting your body properly warmed up and stretched out can help to prevent injuries *before* they happen. Not only is it key to do these things to avoid injuries, but it's also key to performing at your highest level.
- Properly preparing your body is just as much *mental* as it is physical.
- What you eat and drink regularly (especially before competition) plays a significant role in your athletic performance.
- Fruits are a great source of energy that is easier on the digestive system.
- Heavy foods with a lot of fat and grease are not the types of food athletes should consume before a competition.
- Hydration (drinking plenty of water/fluids) is essential to the body.
- Signs of dehydration can include:
    - o Thirst
    - o Sticky or dry mouth
    - o Headache
    - o Dark colored urine
    - o Muscle cramps

- Avoid consuming drinks that have too much sugar.
- Quality sleep habits are critical for athletes to recover and recharge.
- About 8-9 hours of sleep is an excellent range to aim for if possible.
- To increase the quality of sleep, here are things to *avoid*:
  - Sleeping with a light on in the room.
  - Sleeping with noise from a television or other electronics.
  - Eating right before bed.
  - Drinking beverages with caffeine.
- Not getting enough sleep can result in:
  - Lack of concentration
  - Decreased endurance
  - Poor decision making
  - Increased chance of injury
- Never lie about not being injured if you are because you're afraid of what others will think or say.
- Deciding not to take care of an injury properly can prolong it. Listen to your body. Don't ignore unusual pains.
- If you experience an injury, remember:
  - It's not your fault.
  - Things will get better.
  - Don't let fear of injury steal your joy.

- Make a conscious effort to **choose confidence** over fear.
- Awareness of your thoughts and how you use them is essential to managing fear. Constant negative thoughts can contribute to being fearful.
- **Stay Present** - you may neglect to think about the task at hand because you're busy thinking about something that happened (in the past) or hasn't happened (in the future).
- Always have a **"win each play"** mindset.
- If an athlete lets others' perception of them be a determining factor in how they will play, they will always be at a disadvantage. Others' ideas and opinions of you can change as frequently as the weather.
- Be **honest** with yourself about the fears you may have. This honesty is the first step to overcoming fear.

CONCLUSION

Throughout this book, you've been presented with mental and attitudinal elements that can help you become a better all-around athlete. Hopefully, you'll be able to incorporate this information with things you already know. And remember, it's not always what you know; it's whether or not you will use the information provided to motivate and improve yourself as an athlete.

YOU VS. YOU

To be an UNDEFEATED ATHLETE means digging deep within yourself to be the best athlete you can be. It involves setting goals and striving to maximize your ability beyond what you may think isn't possible. It consists of being a leader, a good teammate, and someone that is coachable. It involves taking ownership of your athletic development and not blaming others when you fail. Instead, the UNDEFEATED ATHLETE looks at failure as an opportunity to improve and get better. For the UNDEFEATED ATHLETE, the competition isn't the opponent in front of them; it's the competition within. As mentioned, it's you versus yourself. Before effectively dealing with their opposition, the UNDEFEATED ATHLETE must outcompete who they were yesterday. In all of their practicing and training, they ask themselves:

"CAN I DO BETTER THAN I DID YESTERDAY? CAN I BE BETTER THAN I WAS YESTERDAY?"

THANK YOU

for reading

THE UNDEFEATED ATHLETE:
HOW TO BE A CHAMPION IN ANY SPORT

LEAVE A REVIEW

ON AMAZON.COM

Scan QR code to review

Made in USA - North Chelmsford, MA
1376906_9798218072698
07.17.2023 1654